Infidelity

Infidelity

why men and women cheat

Kenneth Paul Rosenberg, MD

Da Capo
LIFE
LONG

Da Capo Press
Hachette Book Group
1290 Avenue of the Americas, New York, NY 10104
dacapopress.com
@DaCapoPress

Printed in the United States of America
First Edition: May 2018

Published by Da Capo Press, an imprint of Perseus Books, LLC,
a subsidiary of Hachette Book Group, Inc.
The Da Capo Press name and logo is a trademark of The Hachette Book Group.

The Hachette Speakers Bureau provides a wide range of authors for speaking events. To find out more, go to www.hachettespeakersbureau.com or call (866) 376-6591.

The publisher is not responsible for websites (or their content) that are not owned by the publisher.

Editorial production by Christine Marra, *Marra*thon Production Services.
www.marrathoneditorial.org
Book design by Jane Raese
Set in 10.5-point New Baskerville BQ

Library of Congress Cataloging-in-Publication Data has been applied for
ISBN 978-0-7382-2022-2 (hardcover)
ISBN 978-0-7382-2023-9 (e-book)

LSC-C

10 9 8 7 6 5 4 3 2 1

For Claire and Alexander
who guide me, inspire me, and
occasionally, let me parent them

contents

author's note

The patients whose lives I discuss in detail have generously given their permission, and I am completely indebted to each of them. Some of the stories you are about to read also come from people I have known in my personal life. Names and identifying details for all have been changed to protect their privacy. To further disguise the actual patients from my practice, every profile presented in the book is a compilation of at least two, usually three, actual people to ensure that the behaviors of each "book patient" cannot be attributed or linked to any single real, living person. The stories in the book are true and accurate. Nothing in this book should be construed as medical advice, and readers who are wrestling with these issues are urged to seek individualized counseling.

introduction

Not everything that is faced can be changed,
but nothing can be changed until it is faced.

—JAMES BALDWIN

In American society we tend to draw lines between normal and abnormal, sick and well, "sane" and "insane," and the addicted versus those with just a few bad habits. In a similar vein we often think there's a clear division between a "good" spouse and adulterer. I'm here to explain that in reality the differences between these false binaries are not actually so clearly delineated.

Michel Foucault's *The Birth of the Clinic: The Archaeology of Medical Perception* documented how the foundations of Western medicine in the nineteenth century were rooted in such distinctions. The new physicians of the 1800s used their medical gaze to create scientific divisions between normal and diseased states that became critical to our understanding of mental and physical illness. But when it comes to matters of the mind, the lines are actually quite blurry. And when it comes to infidelity, most people live in the gray zone.

The great American psychiatrist Harry Stack Sullivan, MD, was fond of saying that even the sickest mentally ill person is much more like us than different. Nowhere is that fragile line between normal and abnormal more evident than with love and sex. With the right drivers, incentives, and opportunities, any of us can become obsessed with another person. After all, isn't that what falling in love is all about?

Infidelity, defined as a breach in the promise of sexual exclusivity, is the end product of our normal impulses for love and lust gone haywire. Infidelity is a leading cause of divorce in this country. Romantic betrayal can be so devastating that it leads to suicide, homicide, and other crimes of passion. All this, despite the fact that more than 50 percent of "committed" dating people cheat, at least 20 percent of "monogamous" married people cheat, and many of the rest of us supposedly "upstanding citizens" think about it nonstop, although we tend to keep the thoughts to ourselves out of fear of reprisal from our partners and our community. Our adulterous thoughts can sometimes lead us to live in shame, hating ourselves. Although we might tell our partners everything else, our unfaithful thoughts and actions usually remain unspoken. The purpose of this book is to get us thinking about what goes unsaid and to help both adulterers and betrayed spouses alike.

In the pages that follow I quote the scientific literature and explain new discoveries in psychology and neuroscience. I delve into recent findings in genetics that reveal how our genes affect our behavior. I discuss how the new field of epigenetics is demonstrating that not only can our genes affect our behaviors but our behaviors and thoughts can actually change our genes.

My background in treating addiction significantly informs my take on the realities of infidelity. I argue in this book that sex and love are the primordial addictions, meaning our brains evolved to get us addicted to sex and love. These, I argue, are *normal* addictions. If anything can hook you, it's lust and romance! After all, the survival of our species depends on it. But in cases of infidelity this irrational exuberance can bring on a truckload of trouble. Understanding our human frailties does *not* absolve cheaters of responsibility, of course, but it can grant us a new perspective that helps all of us make wiser, more informed choices before we act.

This book is about the role that our brains, our minds (or psychology), and our culture play in infidelity. We'll learn from biological anthropologists and sociologists who have studied the development of infidelity through the course of human evolution. We'll hear from psychologists, who explain how modern times are rife with sexual triggers, and from neuroscientists who understand how our brains betray us. All these experts together offer important perspectives to help explain how and why we get in trouble with sex so that we can learn how to better get a handle on desires that lead to destructive behaviors.

In Part I we will explore the science surrounding sex and infidelity with an intimate glimpse into the brain's reward systems and how they can become hijacked—leading us into destructive behaviors that often include pulling us toward destructive choices, even if we don't actually enjoy them. In Part II we'll discuss the different ways people stray, by and large driven by human tendencies toward seeking novelty. In Part III we'll talk solutions. I'll offer case studies that provide examples of how couples move past an affair. I'll discuss guiding principles to help partners discover their true sexual and romantic potential, unhindered by obstacles like ego and insecurity. And I'll offer practical guidelines to help you avoid—or move out of—the morasses that have ensnared many couples. Although a book about infidelity by nature points out how love and sex can go awry, the take-home message from this book is that passionate love *can* endure despite our innate tendency to cheat and our built-in drive to destroy the good in our lives.

A Little About Me

As a psychiatrist, I am disinclined to talk about myself. Yet before I discuss my patients, I think it's only fair to share a little about how I began working with infidelity. As a young doctor I was thrust into treating philanderers because of my dual interests in the scientific study of sex and my specialization in addiction medicine. (*Philanderer,* by the way, is a term that in common parlance is used to refer to men only. But I'll use it in this book to refer to women too, particularly as *philander* in its Latin derivation implies "lover of men.") Yet long before my professional journey, like many people, my very first experience with infidelity was what I witnessed as a child. This book is not at all about my life, but without a doubt, my own experiences have shaped how I now understand my patients and their families.

My dad co-owned a small meat company in Philadelphia, supplying all the ingredients for Philly's famous steak sandwiches to local restaurants and the food stands along the Atlantic City Boardwalk. As the company salesman, my dad was rarely home, presumably because he was working so hard. My mother was a devoted wife, kind and joyful, and like many white, Jewish, middle-class mothers in the 1960s, she dedicated her entire being to homemaking and childcare. My mother's normal maternal worries were made much worse by the deteriorating mental health of my second-oldest sister, Merle, who slowly devolved from a bright, happy child into a hallucinating schizophrenic person.

During the next decade my wonderful sister's terrible illness plagued her. Merle sought refuge in her room until she could tolerate the hallucinations no longer, and she jumped from her window, three stories above to the concrete pavement.

The fall didn't kill her (although the illness ultimately did), and my beloved sister lived out her life with severe physical and mental limitations. My mother was beside herself with grief and despair. I retreated to my studies and decided to become a psychiatrist to help families like mine. My oldest sister ultimately became a psychologist. Meanwhile my father spent more nights away and, I suspect, sought relief from other women.

I share all this to explain that infidelity exists in a context—in a couple and in a family with its own particular array of hopes and disappointments, triumphs and tragedies. Affairs, new sex, and budding romance can be as much of an escape as drugs and alcohol, and denying affair(s) often reigns supreme. Many families hang onto myths to protect themselves from the truth. In my own family we believed that Dad spent many nights sleeping on the side of the highway. My goal for including this personal information is simply to convey that I both understand how complicated and contextual infidelity is and appreciate how, if my own father could stray, many other decent men and women could easily do the same. As I learned firsthand, infidelity can hit a family like a cluster bomb, perpetually kept a secret and rattling generations to come. On a visceral level many spouses and their children find it impossible to believe, forget, forgive, or reconcile.

Treating philandering spouses became one of my specialties largely by accident. After medical school, medical internship, and a psychiatry residency, during my fellowship at the Cornell Medical Center/New York Presbyterian Hospital, I specialized in sexual disorders and chemical addiction. I studied the early use of Viagra to treat impotence and worked in the field of alcohol, opiate, and cocaine addiction. Early on I was recommended to a public figure who'd had relentless struggles with infidelity. He and his supporters figured that I, an expert in sexual problems (like impotence) and chemical addiction (like alcoholism), could be the one to treat his *sex addiction* and discreetly and effectively extricate him from his personal and public morass.

In the aftermath of a salacious exposé, he came to my office battered and bruised, mocked and humiliated, and in great pain and anguish. His status and family (whom he loved) might never be the same. I treated him well enough and helped him restore his life. But I knew that if I was going to treat more people with sexual compulsivity, I needed more information and experience. So I went to train with the preeminent sex addiction psychologist, Patrick Carnes, PhD.

Largely derided by academics and my fellow psychiatrists, Dr. Carnes was the first psychologist to popularize the term *sex addiction* and quickly became one of my closest colleagues. Around the same time the American Psychiatric Association acknowledged that behaviors such as gambling and, possibly, compulsive internet use could be addictive. Although sex addiction is (still) not accepted as a diagnosis, the new terminology of "behavioral addictions" has enabled psychiatrists to think more expansively about the addictive potential of behaviors involving food and sex. The more I studied with Dr. Carnes, the more I realized that he was onto something potentially lifesaving for my patients. Some years later I was pleased to develop and coedit the first academic book about sexual compulsivity and other behavioral addictions.

The book in your hands is, of course, not a textbook, but it does bring the principles I've learned in science to the human experiences of sex and love. Today we know so much about compulsivity, infidelity, and the science of the brain. By understanding this science, you can begin to understand yourself, your spouse, and your predicament, granting you important tools for managing desires and behaviors so you are not stuck operating at the whim of your emotions and your impulses.

Caveat Emptor

This book contains no easy path to guaranteed happiness; instead, it offers many reasonable paths away from self-destruction. I'm not about to tell you that you can have your cake and eat it too or convince you that your marriage can benefit from affairs that are based on disrespect, lying, and cheating. That's hogwash. What you *won't* find in the following pages are ten easy steps to marital bliss and sexual nirvana.

What you *will* find, however, are clear explanations of the science of how your mind works and how and why affairs develop. I *will* explain how you, your spouse, and even your relationship with one another can survive and even thrive following a secret affair. My patients usually become even stronger as individuals and couples after the discovery of an affair, and I'll tell you how to make that happen. The father of psychoanalysis, Sigmund Freud, wrote that he could treat neurotic misery, but he couldn't save people from *normal* unhappiness. Borrowing from Freud, my job is to rid people not of the normal hiccups and hurdles of relationships but rather of the needless pain and self-torture of cheating.

How do cheaters hurt themselves? The goal of addressing infidelity is not just to promote honesty between spouses but to help us all live lives in accordance with our own ideals. The worst damage that adulterers cause by their infidelity is not only disloyalty to their partner but also betraying themselves through breaking faith with their own hopes and dreams about establishing a trusting, enduring, and loving relationship with someone to whom they've pledged their love.

Whether you've been unfaithful or have discovered the unfaithfulness of your partner, the goal is to help you avoid impulsively and unknowingly destroying your life, your love, and your family. This book is designed to make you an informed owner of your mind and a conscious participant in your sexuality and your relationship as well as to give you the greatest satisfaction through wonderful sex and genuine, sustainable love.

I will present dozens of real-life cases drawn from the stories revealed in my treatment office by people who, other than being unfaithful, are usually good and decent citizens, as well as stories offered by spouses who were betrayed despite being loving and dedicated partners. The details have been anonymized, and the experiences of two or more actual patients have been merged into each single case study to prevent identification and protect patient privacy. All the stories presented are real and not at all exaggerated, and each of the patients discussed in detail generously gave me their permission to use their stories.

Cheating is an equal-opportunity enterprise, affecting people of all socioeconomic groups, races, religions, sexual orientations, and marital arrangements. In this book I use familiar gender names and pronouns (man and woman, he and she), but this content applies equally to different genders as well as to people of various sexual orientations. Although I often use the terms "spouse" and "marriage," readers may fill in their own descriptors for themselves, their partners, and their own particular version of a long-term, committed, romantic relationship. This book even applies to relationships without the prerequisite of monogamy because, as I'll explain in Chapter

1, infidelity has less to do with sex per se and more to do with acts of deception. Therefore, this book is not a diatribe for monogamy. I believe that, with honesty and integrity, people can be happy whether monogamous, nonmonogamous, polyamorous, or even asexual. This book is simply a means to overcome our tendency to deceive and destroy the love in our lives.

Now, let's get to it.

part one

biology and the basics

Most of us think about love, devotion, and sexual desire as a function of our development, parental teaching, background, and early learning. Or even as a function of something strange and hidden, something we can't—and maybe don't even want to—figure out. Scientists, however, have a different view of love, devotion, and sexual desire. They think these emotions largely come from our biology—that evolution created our desires, which are uniquely expressed in different individuals because of other biological and psychological factors. In this section we will explore this argument and try use the science to make some sense of our own bubbling cauldron of feelings around issues of infidelity.

chapter 1

The basics of a cheating heart

We tend to cheat in a haze of delusion, believing that it will bring us real love, help us have better sex, lift our spirits, and boost our sagging self-esteem. Very often, however, cheating ends up wrecking multiple relationships and actually eroding our confidence and sense of self.

We can't say much about infidelity before defining it. *Sexual infidelity* is commonly understood to be a breach in the expectation of sexual exclusivity and can be as slight as a kiss or as significant as intercourse. Experts and researchers usually define infidelity as major sexual transgression, requiring a minimum of genital contact. *Emotional infidelity*, as we'll discuss in Chapter 5, implies an intense emotional bond with a fair amount of sexual tension and desire. Often the most powerful affairs are those that are both emotional and sexual. Studies have repeatedly shown that heterosexual women perceive emotional infidelity to be nearly as threatening to their relationships as physical affairs. Heterosexual men, meanwhile, tend to worry more about sexual betrayals. Gay men and lesbians tend to find sexual and emotional affairs equally distressing, but studies say they are generally less distressed by infidelity than heterosexuals are overall.

Historically speaking, same-gender couples have shown more tolerance for infidelity and tended to recognize a difference between having a sexual tryst and breaking the trust of a committed relationship. Now that same-sex couples are able to legally marry, however, I have witnessed traditional values supplant the more relaxed attitude that my lesbian and gay patients once had about sex outside their primary relationships. In other words, I've noticed in my practice that the gay and lesbian married couples are acting more like straight married couples, with relatively less tolerance of extramarital sex. When surveyed, today's same-gender couples cite a cheating partner as one of the greatest threats to their union.

My patients struggling with infidelity come from a variety of social circumstances and situations—they have different sexual orientations, are at different ages, and come from many religious, racial, and socioeconomic backgrounds. They are millennials who engage in cybersex and have come of age with internet porn, first-date sex, and *friends with benefits*. They are women and men in the midst of midlife crises who fear dwindling opportunities in sex as well as in life in general. They also include the elderly, who are living longer and healthier than ever, confronting changes in their bodies and their desires but enjoying the benefits of drugs and treatments that can enhance their sex lives. I have seen religious people who cheat and people who say they cheat despite the fact that they are happy with their spouses. (In surveys over a third of cheating women and over half of cheating men reported that they were perfectly content with their long-term relationships and cheated despite their satisfaction.)

So who can cheat? Anyone! Anytime! Anyplace! ·

The Three Determinants of Cheating

Over the course of more than two decades in practice I've found three main factors that determine adulterous behavior. They are your:

- brain—the neurological structures and chemistry that evolution gave you
- psychology—the mind that you've developed through formative experiences that imprint certain ways of thinking about the world, your place in it, and how you think about your sexual/romantic self
- culture—the environment around you, with its varying messages about sex, love, and adultery that inform both your opinions about and opportunities for infidelity

Based on studies that we will discuss in the next two chapters, I estimate that nearly 50 percent of what differentiates cheaters from noncheaters has to do with biological differences in their brain chemicals. This means that more than half of what pushes a man or woman to take the plunge to cheat has to do with both one's environment and one's psychology.

The most significant *environmental* cause is the fact that we *can* cheat. The easier it is to do, the more likely we will do it. Cheating is not confined to sleazy people. Under the right circumstances it is very easy to turn lustful thoughts into desperate actions.

As we know from studies of chemical addictions, there are several environmental factors that make bad behaviors more doable. Professionals refer to these as the *three A's*. If a bad behavior is *affordable, accessible,* and *anonymous,* we are more likely to do it. Throughout our discussion here I will repeat and expand on the three A's and how they shape infidelity.

When it comes to the *psychology* of cheaters, the biggest factor driving them to stray is the feeling that they're entitled or deserve to cheat. Research and clinical experience have identified certain personality traits to be associated with this feeling:

1. *Narcissism*—feeling self-entitled and putting one's needs first
2. *Lacking empathy*—not being able to put oneself in another's shoes
3. *Grandiosity*—overestimating one's abilities, especially one's sexual prowess, and needing validation for one's abilities as a lover
4. *Being impulsive*—making important decisions, with major consequences, on the fly
5. *Being a novelty or thrill seeker*—we will devote two chapters to cheaters seeking novel experiences
6. *Having an avoidant attachment style*—fearing commitment
7. *Being self-destructive or masochistic*—a hard-to-grasp psychological concept that I will discuss in detail in the next chapter

What Surveys Tell Us

Infidelity is often cited as the major cause of divorces in the United States, blamed for untold numbers of suicides (particularly among men), and understood to be the root of much unhappiness. But for those who want to stay married after a relationship transgression, it's helpful to know that there is a silver lining to the statistics. Your relationship does not need to end if you can figure out how to communicate and collaborate after the discovery of infidelity.

Although infidelity may be the event that causes a traumatic rupture to the relationship and can throw an unsuspecting partner into despair, it is not the act of infidelity per se that destroys the couple. Rather, relationships end when couples fail to communicate openly, when they struggle with ambivalence about their relationship and lack the commitment to make their marriage work, and when they are unable to bridge the gap after discovering that they have "grown apart." These are the issues that prevent repair and reconciliation after the discovery of affairs, and acknowledging these particular issues is the first step toward resolving them.

There are many statistics about cheating. Here are a few highlights. In 2015 the polling site YouGov surveyed about a thousand Americans and reported that 20 percent of men and 19 percent of women admitted to cheating on their partner. YouGov also reported that roughly 25 percent of individuals (22 percent of men and 27 percent of women) said they have taken back a partner after discovering infidelity. According to a survey of sixty-four thousand individuals, heterosexual men are more likely to be upset by sexual infidelity than heterosexual women (54 percent vs. 35 percent), and women are more likely to be upset by emotional infidelity (65 percent vs. 46

percent). However, gay men and lesbian women were equally likely to be upset by infidelity (32 vs. 34 percent). Among heterosexuals, European men and women are more likely to cheat than Americans. And frequent-flyer business travelers are more likely to cheat than those who don't travel for work. In fact, given that summertime is the peak season for travel, it also becomes a time for new lovers, with the summer months being the peak periods for cheating. Infidelity is not socially sanctioned: 90 percent of adults view sexual infidelity as immoral, and 65 percent view it as unforgivable.

In the past, although male philandering was more acceptable, unfaithful women risked being cruelly ostracized. Economically, psychologically, and socially disadvantaged, women had fewer opportunities to cheat, and even fewer spoke freely about their transgressions. Literature tells stories of women shamed by the scarlet letter ("A" for adulteress), like Hester Prynne, Anna Karenina, and Madame Bovary. But the statistics show that the times are changing.

Since the mid-1970s the General Social Survey of the National Opinion Research Center's (NORC) Center for the Study of Politics and Society has been monitoring attitudes towards sexual behaviors (including infidelity) among a representative sample of nearly thirty-seven thousand Americans. In the late eighties the survey began tracking adulterous behaviors as well. According to their most recent, as-yet-unpublished findings, which may contain the most scientifically reliable infidelity data in the world, the number of married men who have ever cheated has remained stable at around 20 percent from 1993 through 2016. Among women of all ages, however, there is a definite upward trend, from 10 percent of women cheating in 1993 to 15.4 percent today—a rise of roughly 50 percent over the past twenty-four years.

The economic and social emancipation of women, providing more opportunities to cheat in the workplace along with less stigma, are likely reasons for that percentage spike. In general, women have more than leveled the playing field of breaking marital bonds. Years ago it was most often women who were blindsided when their husbands asked for a divorce. Today women initiate divorce roughly 70 percent of the time, with college-educated women initiating an estimated 90 percent of divorces. Interesting to note is the fact that despite increased rates of adultery, the General Social Survey actually shows higher *disapproval* of infidelity today than in the 1970s.

Some researchers report observing a rapid escalation of infidelity among twentysomethings in particular. They have predicted that, with the explosion in internet and cell phone use, cheating rates would skyrocket among younger adults, with rates of adultery among young adult women rising to the level of young adult men. In 2015 other researchers (reporting data that conflicted with the General Social Survey findings) found that women cheated nearly as much as men and reported that infidelity is generally on the rise among both men and women as well as among the young, the middle aged, and seniors. For people over sixty cheating has increased since 1991 by at least 10 percent among women and 14 percent among men.

Statistics and studies are important. However, what I trust most is what I hear from my patients in the privacy of my office, where people tell me things they would never repeat with a researcher. I treat men and women for a variety of problems, not just for cheating or addiction. Regardless of what brings them for treatment, roughly a third of my female patients tell me they have been unfaithful in a relationship. Among my male patients, the surprising reality is that the vast majority has cheated by the age of sixty.

Perhaps I see such high rates of infidelity among patients because I treat a fair number of college-educated people overall. Research confirms that college-educated women, along with those making more than $75,000 a year (particularly women who earn more than their husbands), are more likely to cheat than less educated and less well-off women. I also tend to see people who have loose religious affiliations, although they may go to church, and research confirms that people with weaker connections to their church or religious institutions cheat more. The age demographic among my patients likely has an impact as well. I treat a fair number of middle-aged patients, between the ages of forty and sixty, which is precisely the age range when men and women are most likely to cheat. But I think that the main reason my patients reveal such high levels of infidelity is because they are being *honest.*

We often minimize our dalliances, even to ourselves. We ignore the make-out session with the old flame at the high school reunion. We don't count the affair as cheating if the adulterous relationship turns into a second marriage. We say it didn't count because we were drunk. We say strip clubs and naked women grinding on our genitals till we orgasm didn't count because we were just blowing off steam with the guys. Or we say things like the now-famous words of our philandering former president who allegedly received oral sex (but did not have vaginal intercourse) and defended himself with the lawyerly, "I did not have sexual relations with that woman!"

My Men's Group

"As much as I hate to admit it," says one of the men in my group, "every married man, if he can get away with it, will cheat on his wife every time." Once a week, for several years now, six men—a banker, a stock broker, three doctors, and a real estate salesperson—settle themselves into the soft chairs and black leather couch in my Manhattan office for group therapy, gathering to share stories of compulsive infidelity.

Bob is a banker who wears the typical business-casual uniform: a light-blue blazer and khaki pants. On his first day in the group he told us, "After twelve years of marriage I got bored. I found some unusual things that turned me on. Mostly things my wife wouldn't want to do, or anyway, things I didn't want from her. Dangerous stuff, scary, exciting . . . things that are a little out-of-the-ordinary. One day my wife saw the emails."

The guys in the group nodded their recognition and encouragement. Pete explained his story this way: "After a terrible marriage I finally found my soulmate, Jessica. She's everything I've ever wanted. Then one night, two years after we'd married, don't ask me why, I went on Craigslist and arranged a casual encounter (read: sex) with a random woman. Jessica saw the emails. She freaked. Jess just can't get them out of her head."

Jared is a short, charismatic, curly-haired gay physician who loves his husband, with whom he shares a romantic dream house in rural New Jersey, yet he finds it far too easy to arrange sexual trysts outside his marriage. He says that he could find a sex partner almost anywhere within an hour, adding that he has seduced more than one straight man in his day. He chimed into the discussion with, "Okay, I guess I'm the token gay guy here. But my story is pretty much the same. I'm married to a wonderful, handsome, loving man. But I have a habit—call it a compulsion—of visiting truck stops and upscale department store bathrooms to jerk off with other guys. I always feel like shit when it's over." He looked down and then faced the group. "I need to be a better person. For Stephen. For me."

Charlie told the group that although he has never been even remotely irrational in his business decisions, he's spent hundreds of thousands of dollars on college-aged women whom he's met through SeekingArrangements.com. Sometimes two college students at a time would meet Charlie in a hotel room. Twice he feared they would blackmail him, and once he spent an additional $100,000 to $200,000 to get rid of them. Within a few weeks after he'd paid them off, Charlie started a new batch of "arrangements." To him, this internet-enabled "sex on the side" seemed like a perfect complement to his outwardly respectable life—until his wife discovered the texts, emails, and phone messages. Then "there was hell to pay."

Roger, a big, handsome guy, spoke up next. "Look, who are we kidding? I was born this way! From the first fucking grade, I crawled on my knees—on my knees!—and peeked up my teacher's skirt." He closed his eyes and breathed her in. "And oh my God, what a view!" Roger turned to me. "Dr. Rosenberg, isn't this normal? I mean, we are men! We have urges!"

At the time I offered my reassurance: "There's nothing abnormal about what anyone in this room desires. Most men and women have thought about all of it, at one moment or another. The difference is—and what brought you to this room—that you guys were actually willing to do it!"

Um, Guys? Women Have Urges Too

Although the guys in my men's group might chalk up their transgressions to men being men, the reality is that women have the same desires. And just like men, their urges lead them to stray. Traditionally, women have been understood to crave more romantic fantasies—less aroused by images of naked genitals and more turned on by feelings of being swept off their feet. Research once showed that women who reported not being happy in a relationship were more likely to cheat, while men cheat mostly for the sexual thrill. More recently, however, we've learned that women enjoying new social and cultural freedoms are also excited by visual cues, including porn.

Researchers from the Kinsey Institute and the Center for Sexual Health Promotion at Indiana University in 2011 studied more than a thousand people, half of whom were married and all of whom indicated they were in monogamous relationships. The men in the study were an average age of thirty-three years old, while the average age of the women was twenty-eight. Compared with 19 percent of women, 23 percent of men cheated. The researchers found no statistically significant differences in the reporting of cheating between men and women; however, their reasons for cheating differed. The women studied were more likely to cheat if they felt dissatisfied in their relationships and sought an emotional connection in their affair. Men were more likely to cheat for the sheer excitement of it.

Since 2011 experts continue to report that younger women are cheating in numbers similar to men. Although today's women are more likely to cheat than their mothers were, the reasons for their cheating have stayed the same: first, to seek a connection they feel is lacking in their relationship, and second and perhaps more than ever before, to remedy sexual boredom.

Laura, a forty-two-year-old mother of two with a master's degree in fine arts that she wasn't using and who spent enormous amounts of time on social media, fit the profile reflected by current statistics suggesting that computer-savvy women with advanced degrees are more likely to cheat. Ten years into

her marriage Laura was feeling lonely, unfulfilled, unappreciated, and suffered from low self-esteem when she found love
with the man who operated the elevator in their building.

As often happens, Laura's idealization of her once-beloved
husband turned into devaluation and even vilification. "He's a
pig," Laura told me. "He doesn't wash. He sleeps on the floor."
This description was hard to reconcile with the fact that he
was a respected doctor who was loved by his patients. But I've
learned that over time many married couples wind up viewing their spouses with what I jokingly refer to as "shit-tinted
glasses." It never ceases to amaze me the way a former true
love can suddenly come to be seen as a total heel, but it happens over and over again.

By contrast, Laura found the "elevator man" to be handsome, muscular, well kept, courteous, and chivalrous. He
smelled good and listened empathically to her concerns.
During his workday they exchanged stolen kisses in the elevator. During his days off they retreated to his favorite bar and
made love in the back room.

"Why don't you just leave your husband, Laura?" I asked.
But she had seen vicious divorces among her friends and worried about her young children. Plus, her husband had fallen
apart when she had left once before. Laura decided that for
her the right move was to tough it out for at least a couple
more years.

Life Circumstances That Lead to Cheating

As we will discuss throughout the book, studies tell us there
are associations between cheating and life situations. There is
conflicting data about the impact of age, with some surveys

claiming forty-nine to be the peak age of male cheating, other studies claiming thirty-nine years of age for both men and women, and some claiming twenty-five to thirty-five years of age as the peak female cheating years. Personally, I think the risk is more dependent on commonsense factors like how long a couple has been married, where they are in their careers and with raising children, what their health and hormonal levels are like at various ages, and what is happening to them and among their peers in their community at any particular phase in their life cycle.

One of the more fascinating contributions to understanding sex comes from emerging studies in neuroscience. Many marriage and relationship experts don't understand the biology very well but nonetheless apply the results from a few rat studies to humans and, as a result, exaggerate the findings. Other experts, meanwhile, do the opposite: they ignore the studies and call them "uninteresting" because the neuroscience is beyond their understanding. Some people seem to find the idea that chemicals determine your behavior to be creepy and hate the notion that their motivations can be understood by a set of predictable chemical reactions occurring in the brain. But the new neuroscience of sex and monogamy is fascinating. It's worth understanding, and, I promise, I'll make it easy to follow.

Our Sexual Brains: A Preview

"Anatomy is destiny," wrote Sigmund Freud in his 1912 paper on the nature of romantic love. Freud was a strong believer that gender determined our thoughts and desires. Now, more than a hundred years later, scientists have found evidence of the actual biological mechanisms that contribute to our sexual desires.

We will discuss these findings in the next two chapters. You will learn that we are born with genetic factors that cause chemical changes and influence our sexual thoughts and behaviors. A second and maybe even more interesting piece of new information is that not only do your genes influence your behavior, but also your behaviors and thoughts can actually change your genes and your brain.

We have feedback loops—interconnections between biology, psychology, and culture—and when we experience a certain successful pattern of behavior for getting sex, it can forge a pathway in our brain, creating a channel we travel over and over. These paths become deeply ingrained in our gray matter (where our brain cells, or neurons, reside) and act as favored patterns for our actions. Memories become physiologically locked in our minds through chemical reactions. **Like a path in an overgrown forest, how we think about, seek out, and ultimately find sex creates a biological imprint in our brains,** and it becomes difficult to venture off the established way that has brought us so much pleasure.

Jake's story: The mechanisms of sexual memory

Forty-five-year-old Jake came to see me because he was in crisis about his infidelity. Some five years earlier the mere thought of cheating on his wife had been abhorrent to him. On occasion he would wake in the middle of the night in a cold sweat, jolted awake by a nightmare in which he'd had sex with a woman other than his wife. His older brother had been a philanderer, and Jake wanted never to be like him. Jake hung onto his fidelity as a badge of honor and dreaded the day when he might be tempted to stray.

Jake suffered from anxiety and narcissism. Although Jake and his wife had sex regularly, he said his wife showed him little affection. When Jake longed for the tender touch of a woman, he went for massages at a local spa. Unlike many men in his neighborhood in Queens—said to be the epicenter of New York City's sex trafficking business—Jake never dreamt of asking for a "happy ending," the euphemism for ending a massage by masturbating a man to orgasm. The tender touch and nurturing of a woman was all he desired, something like the comforting touch of his mother when he was a child.

Jake loved the massages and felt resigned to a loveless marriage. The trouble started when he suffered a serious personal loss. I've seen over and over again how men often self-medicate their emotional pain with sexual infidelity. In fact, more men in my practice have begun cheating soon after the death of a parent than following any other major life event. Jake was no exception. Literally on the day his mother lay dying in the hospital, he arranged for a sexual massage. Although he knew that most of the Asian women who worked at these spas were working under the thumb of intimidation, no concern for their circumstances entered his mind. Nothing could sway his determination. As soon as he was on the massage table he placed the masseuse's hand on his penis. Surprised, she asked him, "What do you need?" "You . . . I need you," Jake replied, and they locked eyes. For a $40 tip, his masseuse became his lover.

Memories are simply persistent chemical reactions that maintain changes in the synapses—the connections between neurons—in the brain. When we have an important experience, new proteins are made at the synapses. In particular, a protein called PKMzeta triggers the strengthening of a synapse and, boom, a memory is born and sustained over time. When a sexual or fear-associated memory is formed, the brain becomes flooded with high levels of neurotransmitters—serotonin, dopamine, and epinephrine—that act like fertilizer to increase the activation of the neurons. This activation increases the power of

continues

the memory. Memories that are associated with emotion are stored in a part of the brain called the *amygdala,* a tiny, nut-sized area that acts like a fortress to keep those important memories strong and secure.

Unfortunately, Jake's new sexual memory was now secure in the vault, powered by a combination of desire and shame. He hated himself for his indiscretions, yet his longing and sadness kept him coming back. This set the stage for the beginning of the end of his intimacy with his wife. His infidelity made him feel more alone, ashamed, and angry. He now had major internal conflicts about his unfaithfulness that he couldn't share with his wife. He felt entitled to the sweet, sexual massages and justified them in his own mind by his wife's coldness. His emotions impaired his judgment when dealing with her. He was furious one minute, solicitous the next. He never confessed, but after a few tortuous years Jake called out his wife on her coldness, demanding that they have love in their lives. Now it was too late to fix it. Jake's wife shut down completely. Soon thereafter the couple divorced.

After that, Jake self-medicated his loneliness and loss by bedding as many women as he could. He started and broke off relationships as the spirit moved him, with little consideration for the feelings of the women he was using. When he finally realized that he wanted a committed relationship—which would prove impossible unless he started behaving differently—he sought treatment. Jake had been using women to validate himself and improve his low self-esteem. We discussed how similar this was to his experiences in the massage parlors. I soon worked out a treatment plan:

1. medication to decrease the anxiety that drove him to soothe himself with sex
2. meditation to quiet and focus his mind .
3. group therapy with like-minded men to help him problem solve and feel less alone
4. rules for conduct in relationships

chapter 2

Desire: The engine of the affair

Long-term relationships are usually predicated on some degree of initial sexual chemistry: the body parts move well together; a partner's scent or touch sends shivers. Their looks excite us from afar and drive us wild up close. The feel and fit electrify beyond words. We feel desire. Ultimately the important determinants of relationship longevity, as both research and my clinical experience confirm, include shared values, mutual respect, and, most importantly, developing a stable partnership free of needless drama and conflict. But without some chemistry, in the beginning at least, a romantic relationship is unlikely to ever blossom into a long-term relationship.

Affairs are also about chemistry. In fact, most people would say that the physical chemistry of the affair is the most important element because there is little sharing of familial duties and less time for chitchat. No time for long dinners, quiet evenings on the couch after the kids are asleep, or social engagements with family or friends. The supercharged rendezvous of an affair often centers around sex, leaving aside other typical coupledom activities. So, naturally, sexual affairs are more about sexual chemistry than long-term relationships are, right?

Absolutely not. In truth, affairs usually involve spending less time with an actual, real, live human and more time with the person that we've conjured up from our yearnings, our hopes, our fantasies and fears, and from what psychiatrists call our "internal representations" of another. **Affairs are actually built not in the bedroom but in the mind.** Concocted in our irrationally exuberant and sometimes desperate imaginings, affairs draw their power from deep wants and needs. Their magnetism has its roots in desire.

Desire Is Key

An average couple engages in sex for under six minutes. Men's orgasms last for less than five seconds on average. Women's orgasms, meanwhile, vary from three seconds to three minutes, with the average estimates ranging from roughly ten to twenty seconds. As it turns out, **much of what we consider sex is not about arousal and orgasm but rather desire.** Sex lasts minutes. Orgasms last seconds. But we can maintain our fantasies for a lifetime. Fantasy is the flame of passion. Desire has a way of getting us engaged, keeping us in a zonked-out zone, getting lost in lust and love, and, in some cases, blinding us to self-destructive choices.

My thinking about desire was transformed early in my career by the work of my former professor and mentor Helen Singer Kaplan, MD, PhD, founder of the first clinic in the United States for the treatment of sexual disorders and author of the 1979 book *Disorders of Desire*. Dr. Kaplan was among the first academics to highlight the importance of desire and examine it through medical and academic study.

Dr. Kaplan's 1977 paper on low sexual desire broke new ground by exploring the motivational aspects of sex that previous studies had neglected. Pioneers of sex research and treatment in the 1950s and 1960s, William H. Masters and Virginia E. Johnson (known commonly as Masters and Johnson), had focused exclusively on what happened *in* the bedroom—namely the immediate excitement phase of sex (known as the arousal stage) and orgasm. They ignored how the couple wound up in bed together. Masters and Johnson helped men with erectile dysfunction (can't get a hard-on), premature ejaculation ("cum" too quickly), retarded ejaculation ("cum" too slowly), and retrograde ejaculation ("cum" backward into the bladder). They helped women with anorgasmia (no orgasm) and vaginismus (vaginal spasms preventing penetration). In contrast to their psychoanalytic predecessors, who focused on years of treatment through exploring the unconscious, Masters and Johnson came up with behavioral exercises, bypassing unconscious drives and problems.

At first Dr. Kaplan did the same, but soon she discovered that a lot of her patients had problems stemming not from the mechanics of sex but from the lack of desire, and that these problems preempted and prevented a satisfying sex life.

Although she felt desire disorders were deeply rooted in the mind and thus might require years of psychoanalysis to uncover, she developed techniques and approaches to shortcut the unconscious and get the patient on the road to healthy sex and lustful desire. Dr. Kaplan created many techniques based on this first, most vital stage of sex. Of her many interventions, what helped her patients with desire issues the most was talking openly and honestly to explore their innermost and often secret wants and urges. As any experienced lover can confirm, speaking truthfully and then being accepted without judgment is good for sex.

Today psychology and medical professionals affirm Dr. Kaplan's conclusion that the desire phase, deeply rooted in the psyche and the most psychologically complex, is the most pivotal.

A few years before she died, one late afternoon in our classroom at Cornell Medical Center, Dr. Kaplan was working on the revision of her book on desire. She asked us, her trainees, to list all the desire disorders we could think of for her new edition. I suggested one: "Hypersexuality," I said quietly. Dr. Kaplan politely added "hypersexuality" to her list on the blackboard. But I could tell that she didn't really believe for a moment that too much libido was frequently a bad thing.

Dr. Kaplan had come of age in a time of sexual liberation and revolution—at a time when homosexuality was still considered a disease. When women never discussed masturbation. When all female orgasms were thought to arise from missionary-position vaginal intercourse. She and her colleagues had been the ones to teach us that female orgasms arose from stimulation of the clitoris, which sits at the top of the vulva just above the vagina, not the vaginal canal itself.

Given the repression and ignorance she combated, whatever promoted more safe sex was a good thing in her book. *Too much sexual desire* must have struck her as a throwback to the anachronistic thinking from when she'd grown up. It's odd that I remember this one moment so well. The memory has most likely endured because it was the only time I can recall when my brilliant teacher, who made us realize the vital role of desire, was wrong. As it turned out, thirty years later many of the patients I see complain that they have *too much desire.*

Desire for Another Tribe Member

For humans who live and die to realize their desires, the first order of evolution was to make us want and pursue mates who would be good for the survival of our species. Our DNA contains about twenty thousand genes encoded in forty-six chromosomes—twenty-three that we get from our mothers and twenty-three from our fathers. If one of our parents has a damaged gene, the other parent usually has a good copy of the gene to make up for it. That is (one of many reasons) why mating with a sibling is ill-advised, because it creates offspring who lack a back-up gene for any damaged ones, increasing the chances of giving birth to a child with a fatal disease. This idea of diversifying our gene pool is key to understanding the evolutionary role of desire: the more diversified our children's genes, the healthier our offspring will be. Bottom line: our brains evolved to lust after those who are different from our blood relatives in order to prevent sick children and to diversify and improve our genetic codes. Genetic diversity is good for the human species, making us taller, healthier, and smarter.

Although we are prohibited from marrying siblings and rarely marry cousins, we often marry within the same tribe, within the same religion, coupling with people with similar customs and values who grow up in similar geographical regions. We most often feel more comfortable and wind up paired with people who are like us. But desire is another matter.

When it comes to desire, the familiar is not a turn-on. In many replicated studies, heterosexual women and men sniffed the T-shirts of several anonymous gender-opposite people and chose which ones they felt were the sexiest. Overwhelmingly the participants selected T-shirts of the people who were genetically different from them in a specific part of the immune system called the *major histocompatibility complex* (MHC). This preference was telling because when couples with genetic similarity in the MHC reproduce, that similarity can sometimes lead to complications in fertility and pregnancy.

So by and large, we end up *married* to people from our tribe but *lust* after people from other tribes. One study found that women married to men with similar genes in the MHC had more affairs. In fact, the more genes she shared with her spouse in the MHC, the more extramarital partners she coupled with. Remarkable, right?

There is a plausible genetic and immunological explanation for why we are attracted to people who are different from us: mating with someone from a different gene pool results in diversity in the newborn's genes that may help prolong survival by boosting the immune system and lessening the likelihood of a genetically transmitted disease. Our brains developed to incorporate this evolutionary need and, subsequently, evolved to fool us into doing evolution's bidding while thinking that we are just following our deep-seated, soul-fulfilling lusts.

Novelty Creates Desire—The New Rat in the Cage

Newness is intoxicating, literally. In fact, the pursuit of novelty is one of the most basic, primitive desires, has been demonstrated in a multitude of different species, including rats.

Drop a male rat into a cage with a female rat who's in heat, and the two will copulate repeatedly until sexual exhaustion. Drop a brand *new* rat into the cage and, despite the other rats' exhaustion, both male and female rats will rally to resume mating activity with the new partner. The new rat in the cage gets all the attention, despite the original rat's disinterest in any additional sex with the previous mate. This phenomenon (called the Coolidge effect after a joke about then-President Calvin Coolidge and his wife) is an ancient biological program aimed at seizing genetic opportunities, driven by a neurological mechanism whereby potent brain chemicals jolt a "sexually satiated" animal to continue to copulate. The appeal of a new mate over a pre-existing mate can be seen in both males and females up and down the phylogenetic spectrum, from beetles to primates.

Like most instinctual behaviors, the Coolidge effect is exquisitely programmed in the brain. The desire for novelty can be attributed by dopamine release in the *nucleus accumbens* and *ventral tegmental area*, which serve as a crucial link in an animal's limbic system, also known as its reward/reinforcement center. When an animal spots food or opportunities for sex, the nucleus accumbens responds to these important cues by releasing the neurotransmitter dopamine, which reinforces and orients the brain toward attaining these species-preserving priorities.

Many of my patients stray despite having spouses whom they desire and with whom they often enjoy great sex lives.

They stray despite the fact that they are already paired with perfectly good mates. And if and when they divorce, the mate they dismissed like yesterday's bad news becomes someone's new perfect find. This is precisely what happened to Laura, who wound up disgusted by the man who had once been her beloved groom and idolized the elevator man who, quite likely, was not the apple of his last partner's eye. I call this the *musical chairs of desire*. One mate's nightmare becomes the next mate's dream come true.

Often my patients succumb to each new opportunity or, to put it more crudely, each new rat in the cage. Even the men in my practice who pay for sex from prostitutes, masseuses, or through online sugar daddy "arrangements" rarely hire the same person again and again. They're forever seeking someone new. Affairs of the heart and journeys of sexual desire take over the reward centers of your brain, and new sex and love further cloud or subvert the decision-making abilities of your brain's frontal lobes.

Thrill Creates Desire

Somehow it became a popular myth that men think about sex every seven seconds. I'm not sure anyone thinks about sex every seven seconds, but generally speaking, we think about sex quite a bit, although typically less than we think about sleep and food. (Studies conclude that, actually, we mostly think about our next meal.) Researchers at Ohio State University found that male college students, on average, think about sex nineteen times a day, and female college students think about sex ten times a day. Naturally, some people have sex on their minds more than others. Among the 283 college students studied, one thought about sex only three times in one day, and another thought about it 388 times in a day. What is clear to me from my patients is that in some cases the thoughts about having sex with someone other than a primary partner can be more titillating than the actual experience. Before I introduce more of my patients, there's one more experiment that helps us understand what makes cheating lovers tick.

One reason cheaters find affairs so enticing is precisely because they are secret and forbidden. The transgression itself is actually part of the draw—at least until guilt sets in. For decades social scientists have recognized the tendency for adrenaline to make the heart grow fonder. In 1974 two well-known psychologists, Arthur Aron and Donald Dutton, devised a seminal experiment to explore the nature of sexual attraction known as the Shaky Bridge Study.

Two bridges crossing a river in Canada set the stage for a two-part experiment. The first bridge was the five-foot-wide, 450-foot-long suspension bridge constructed of wood planks and cable, which swayed in the wind 250 feet above rocks and water. The second was an anchored bridge sitting solidly just 10 feet above sea level. In the experiment each unaccompanied man who stepped off either the shaky bridge or the solid bridge was approached by a woman offering her name and phone number.

Researchers found that the men who had crossed the shaky bridge were more likely to accept the phone number, call the woman, and ask her out on a date. When subsequently asked why, the men "misattributed" their physiological arousal from the anxiety, fear, or excitement of crossing the shaky bridge as sexual attraction. Instead of taking into account the charge in their nervous system from the terrifying bridge, they explained that the woman excited them, not realizing that the arousal they felt actually had little to do with her. Experimentally matched men who had just crossed a calm bridge found the female at the other end significantly less exciting.

This finding is highly instructive for any of us looking to better understand how our brain's reward systems can override our rational side if we're not paying attention. More often than we might realize, we find ourselves experiencing sensations of arousal, then searching our environments for a potential cause. Social scientists call this *misattribution of arousal*. And keying into its effects might just prompt the second-guessing of one's own responses that could prevent a life-altering transgression.

The most important take-home lesson here is that desire often has more to do with your own feelings, your mental representations of another, and the context of your encounter than with the desired person him or herself. Getting turned on is less about the other person than it is about the inner workings of your own mind. When you meet a new lover you say, "I don't know—he just excites me in a way my husband just can't. I just married the wrong man!" You ignore the adrenaline of this forbidden chance encounter, the uncertainty of his desire for you, the pulse of the new music, the exotic new cocktail you've ordered, and the unseen corners at the darkened bar. Instead, you attribute your desire to the new person. You compare him to your old husband sitting in front of a bright television screen, the remote in his hand, maybe asleep and snoring, with food stains on his boxers. You forget that you're meeting this new person on a kind of shaky bridge. Although you might not realize it, the thrill of the new, fueled by the brain's novelty-seeking chemicals, is making your heart grow fonder.

Anthony's story: Locked in the spaceship

Fifty-three-year-old Anthony liked to say that sex for him was like co-caine for an addict. "I've always had a huge sex drive," he explained when he came to me for treatment. During one of our group ther-apy sessions Anthony shared something that he'd heard a famously drug-addicted sports figure say: doing cocaine made him feel like he'd boarded a rocket ship that catapulted him into outer space. Get into the spaceship, press a button, and away he'd go. There was no turning him back from his mission. That's just what *desire* did for *him*, Anthony explained.

Once Anthony started on his path, turning on a computer to look for sex sites, he was past the point of no return. It took him into an altered state and propelled him into an alternative universe. He be-came like a person locked in a spaceship; his mind would not let him out. Instead, desire and sexual fantasy kept him in a trance, intent on his mission. All the men in my Monday group nodded their agree-ment. Like most humans, been there, done that.

As someone whose testosterone level ran naturally high, Anthony was biologically primed for greater sexual interest and arousal. This fact was compounded by the circumstances of his upbringing, and he'd been captivated by sex for as long as he could remember. Our first sexual longings determine much of the course of our entire lives, according to Freud. For Anthony, this certainly seemed to be the case. As a child he'd shared a bedroom with a makeshift wall with his sister and used to peek at her as she undressed.

Later, as a youth, Anthony's hypercharged sexual urges did not find a ready outlet among his peers. He was not popular with girls and had virtually no dating experience. He became a bit of a "peeping tom." By his twenties Anthony's brain had combined the forbidden

continues

fruits of his childhood, the thrill of the hunt, and the adrenaline rush that the experimental subjects felt on the bridge.

I know Anthony to be a good man—hardworking, a compassionate boss, a great father and loving husband, a pillar in his community, and extremely ethical. As happens with many people, sex is the one area where his otherwise stellar ethics and morality fell apart. Anthony was deeply in love with his wife and never allowed himself to touch another woman. What Anthony loved was thinking about sex with other women, shutting the door to his office and fantasizing about a potential affair partner. Anthony was a desire junkie.

Anthony had such a strong active imagination that just thinking about sex would put him in the zone. Even at work he'd wind up masturbating. As Mondays were particularly stressful, he was more likely to do it then. He could get completely lost in fantasy.

Over time, as the fantasies drove him to touch himself, that physical contact created an even stronger feedback loop between his brain and his genitalia. This circuit, strengthened by the frequency of his habit, would drive him into a frenzy of desire that threatened his reputation and compromised his time. And when it was all over, Anthony, like many of my male patients, felt disgusted with himself. Masturbation at work was just one of the multiple ways that sexual thoughts and actions were causing trouble for Anthony. He was ready to change. But how?

The Brain Under a Microscope at Orgasm

Our brains are programmed by millions of years of evolution to seek sex and love with life-and-death desperation. But male and female brains appear to operate differently in the courtship and arousal period. Recently researchers in the

Amelia's story: "I will never sleep with you again"

When she was twenty-five years old, Amelia, a conservative WASP from the Midwest, was married for less than six months when she met a debonair, slightly older African American man at the bank where she worked. She was a teller, and he, a bank manager. After work he'd take her to his place, cook her dinner, then sit her down and provide her with oral sex. She would relish his attention and then make her way home to her husband in Yonkers. The forbidden rendezvous was quite a turn-on. The relationship lasted a few months—until she got bored of the novelty. She told me that she only strayed because she felt afraid that her husband might one day cheat on her, and this was her way to get even beforehand. But it seemed to me that Amelia was just looking for a way to justify her lust. As it turned out, her husband never strayed and was devoted to her throughout the marriage, leaving her with the guilt of her novelty-seeking transgression.

Amelia and her husband shared the same religion, the same friends, and the same political values. Together they raised four children. Yet, just as so many other women have told me, Amelia explained that she is not sure why she married her husband. Many of the women I've treated marry men who they think will be good providers and will help create safe and stable homes. They are men who won't stay out too late or seek out other women in bars. They treat their wives with respect and kindness. They are men who are respected in their community, can be counted upon in a pinch, and will always stay true blue. Unfortunately, for Amelia and so many other women, after a couple of decades of marriage their rocks of Gibraltar become insufferably boring.

Near her fiftieth birthday Amelia decided there must be more to life than her dull husband. She told him, "I will never sleep with you again" and meant it. It devastated him, and she took up with a new

continues

man she met on a dating site. Her new beau was someone from a different part of the country, with a different religion, different political beliefs, and an unstable and wild sexual energy that was completely the opposite of her predictable husband. She was the WASP, and he was a Bohemian Jew.

Amelia was completely turned on by her new mate and happily divorced her husband of twenty years. Once she started seriously dating her new boyfriend, however, she discovered that although he turned her on to no end, the differences in their styles and beliefs made life together intolerable. Amelia could never give him up yet could not stay engaged with him. Their tortured love affair went on for four years until he finally married someone else.

Amelia realized it was time for some deep therapy. She decided that she would need to look at her boredom and relationships with men. In therapy we have an opportunity to lay out our struggles with our biological drives and delve deeply into the psychological forces that influence us. In therapy Amelia discussed the trauma of her own parents' divorce, the impact of watching her parents' dysfunctional relationship, her history of complicated relationships with men, and her hopes for a loving romantic life. Amelia had everything going for her, except now she needed to get her mind in order. The first step was to understand her brain.

Netherlands studied men and women in brain scanners while having sex with their partners. The typical guy got turned on by what he saw (which is mediated by the activation of his visual cortex) and by what he imagined his orgasm would be like (which is mediated by his brain's reward center).

When the women felt desire, however, more was happening in their brains. Not only were the reward centers activated, but there was also activation of the frontal and auditory lobes that are important in empathic listening and assessing the overall suitability of a mate. These brain studies suggested that, even in the throes of lovemaking, women might be more attuned to finding a relationship partner than just having good sex. This finding raises the question: In societies where women are now much less dependent on men, are women still so relationship focused?

Evolutionary scientists believe that men and women developed different brain-based instincts in order to ensure the survival of the species. Regardless, we are in the midst of a turning point. Women in the 1970s cheated a fraction as much as their male counterparts. If current trends continue, within a decade young adult women will cheat as much as young adult men. Have we reached a point in our evolution in which women can be less fidelity focused? Do women no longer need to constantly evaluate the viability and feasibility of their partner? And, therefore, can twenty-first-century women behave more like twentieth-century men?

Nearly twenty years ago HBO asked me to lead an online discussion about their hit series *Sex and the City*. At the time I felt that rather than depicting a typical representation of most women at the time, the female characters on *Sex and the City* showed predatory and genitally oriented sexual behavior that was much more typically *male*. Now I believe that the behaviors displayed on that television show actually foreshadowed a shift in our society. Today, for better or for worse, more women are acting more like men. Based on both research and my clinical experience, many women feel empowered to seize the freewheeling sexual mantle that had previously belonged mainly to men.

Today we find young women emulating many of the patterns of male cheating, which focus on genital arousal as

opposed to the more "typically female" interest in an emotional connection. The younger women I treat in my practice
express far more desire for sex with no emotional strings attached than older women do. Twenty years ago commercial
sex-oriented activities were rare among women, but now it's
far more common for bachelorette parties to include a trip
to a male strip club, for example. Sex clubs for women have
never been popular, but now OMing (orgasmic meditation),
developed by women, is a national "club" in which women go
to have a ritual clitoral massage performed by men who are
often strangers.

Inevitably, cultural and psychological shifts will affect how
women behave sexually. And because we now know that experiences, culture, and psychology can "turn on" new gene products in the brain, we can expect changes in the sexual brains of
women in the generations to come.

Before we leave this introductory chapter on the biology of
desire, there's one more concept we need to address: the major neurological connection for sex, otherwise known as the
reward center of your brain.

Meet Your Reward Center

All this desire stuff we are talking about occurs at a completely
unconscious level. We are responding to evolution, biological imperatives, and psychological experiences—all operating
without our awareness. The place where this happens is the
reward center of our brains.

Let me introduce you to the middle of your brain. Dopamine
is the fuel of your reward center. It is the "feel-good" chemical
that we will discuss in detail in the next chapter. Other key

chemicals involved in your reward center include adrenaline and noradrenaline (their medical names are epinephrine and norepinephrine), which summon a state of urgency, as well as the chemical brain bath of male and female hormones called testosterone and estrogen, which make your brain desire sex. Your reward center has an opiate system called endorphins. (Yes, you have something like heroin floating in your head.) Your brain also has its own marijuana chemicals called endocannabinoids. (Yes, pot is legal in your brain!) Your opiate and marijuana reserves play a central role in your sexual desire, but more important are the chemicals that make you feel attached to your spouse and children, the chemicals of bonding, called oxytocin and vasopressin. Now, that's a quick introduction. See how cool your brain is? We'll explore in the next chapter exactly how these chemicals work.

chapter 3

Sex and love:
The primordial addictions

*The human species developed dual reproductive strategies.
The tremendous drive to pair up as a couple and rear at least
one single child as a team, and an opposing drive towards
clandestine adultery and our predispositions to mate with
many folks to procreate and diversify our gene pool because
those offspring, with diverse genes, survive best.*

That's how biological anthropologist Helen Fisher sums up
her forty years of researching more than forty cultures. In this
chapter I will simplify decades of research about these dual

mandates: the urge to cheat and the urge to connect. Each of us has a brain primed for lust and immediate sexual gratification while it is also ready for long-term coupling. Your culture, your religion, your values, your intentions—in sum, your psychological and spiritual selves—are of paramount importance in shaping the decisions you make that determine your behavior. But you don't underestimate the power of your brain. Here's why . . .

The Brain Makes Sex Salient

Salience is a term used in addiction medicine, and it accounts for why the addict becomes obsessed with their mission—why, once they get into the addicted state-of-mind, once they enter the spaceship, they can't be deterred from their mission to obtain their drug of choice. In drug addiction salience means that the addict's quest to get their fix trumps reason and overrides yesterday's regret. They will steal, lie, cheat—do whatever it takes to get their drug.

Because infidelity involves our primitive drives, the urge to cheat has salience. It means that a person's brain becomes focused on and mobilized around a desire, however irrational. When the urge to cheat has salience for a person, then cheating overshadows reason, and straying moves to the top of the list of the many good and bad ideas we have.

During salience the memory part of the brain, the *hippocampus*, compares the imagined encounter—be it sexual or emotional—to prior sexual or emotional experiences. The nucleus accumbens, the brain's equivalent to Grand Central Station for the reward and pleasure pathways, gets our brain (and body) juices flowing. The brain chemical of desire, dopamine, bathes the brain cells and provides the gas for the engine to stay lustful. Another brain chemical, adrenalin, keeps the mind and body running in high gear and creates a feedback loop of urgency, despite that no real urgency for mating still exists—at least as far as survival of the species is concerned. This cascade of chemical reactions focuses the mind on the new playmate(s), creating a psychological vortex of hope and lust that make the desire stronger. That's salience.

Salience occurs at an unconscious, neurochemical level and varies in intensity from person to person and situation to situation. Depending on how strongly aroused we are, salience can range from being a faint feeling to an overwhelming yearning. In most of the cases presented in this book, the desire for the affair-partner was strong enough to have become salient.

How is it that salience enables the reward center to take over the mind? After all, we have frontal lobes, our reasoning part of the brain, to get us to think logically and not just follow whatever looks, feels, and tastes good. The answer is that over time the pursuit of "rewarding" behavior alters the frontal cortex that guides our behaviors, gives us consciousness, and enables us to know right from wrong.

So how then does the irrational mission happen? Desire hijacks the brain through chemical reactions in the reward center that convince the frontal lobes to agree to the misguided plan. In the case of drug addiction, scientists have identified how the addicted brain develops new chemical alterations in the frontal lobes that reprogram the reasoning center to become *un*reasonable. The evolutionarily older parts of the brain (sometimes referred to as our reptile brain because they're our brain's most basic primitive areas) control the reward system and persuade the newer logic systems of the brain, such as the frontal lobes, to go along for the ride. (By the way, by "newer" I mean only about two million years old, versus five hundred million years ago, when the first worms appeared, and two hundred million years ago, when the first mammals appeared on earth.)

Currently no scientific studies of the brain conclusively demonstrate that lustful desire changes the brain in the way we know happens with drug addiction. However, it is my opinion that the very same process occurs with sexual desire. Scientists who study sexual arousal and social bonding have found that the powerful biological forces at work are similar to what happens with addiction. In fact, I believe that drug addiction is only possible because the drug of choice takes the place of love and sex. Cocaine and heroin are tapping into our normal reward systems that evolution put into place to get us hooked on love, sex, food, and other basic biological urges that promote the survival of the species. As you'll soon hear from experts, the brain's addictive centers were created to get us addicted not to cocaine or heroin but rather to the essential ingredients for the survival of our species: food, sex, and love. When people ask me, "Really? We can be addicted to sex?!" I reply, "If there's anything the brain can become addicted to, it would be sex."

Sex: The Primordial Addiction

I often think that the difficulty we have in thinking about love and sex as addictive has to do with semantics. Addiction is a name that we in the twentieth and twenty-first century call an unhealthy lust. Such a construct implies a disease process. But the brain doesn't pay any mind to these concepts. The brain doesn't care if you call it addiction or romance. The brain operates based on certain principles and drivers. Desires drive us, and we sometimes watch ourselves on our mission with sheer disbelief.

This connection to the brain's reward centers that can get us in trouble with lust also sustains our love with a primary partner and helps maintain a long-term relationship. Researchers in labs around the globe have used brain-imaging technology to show which areas of the brain light up when people look at photos of their romantic partners. They have found that the same areas of the brain that become active when addicts crave their drugs of choice fire up when people experience romantic yearning. The brain scans showed activity in regions rich with the neurotransmitter dopamine—zones associated with pleasure, focused attention, and reward detection as well as the motivation to pursue and acquire rewards.

Wanting but Not Liking

With addiction it's clear: we seek a drug or pursue a behavior (like overeating), and we feel unable to reasonably control or manage our cravings. With sex and love our desires also feel beyond our control or choice. As Anthony explained, for him it was like getting into a spaceship, the door shutting, and immediately getting zonked out into the zone. With sex we sometimes know that what we are about to do is wrong, yet we still feel lost in that zone. This is not just true of sex or love addicts—people destroying their lives with dysfunctional and destructive relationships—but also common to many people who end up having sex at the wrong time, in the wrong place, and with the wrong people. I want to now speculate on the neurophysiology and psychology of one such patient.

About one year into our treatment Matthew had a few hours to kill before he had to be at work. This was always a risky time for Matthew. He had just finished a good morning psycho-therapy session where we had discussed his sincere love for his new girlfriend. We also talked about how, now that he was involved in a committed relationship and the uncertainty of the chase was no longer there, he was becoming less sexually attracted to her. Matthew was now at risk for committing infi-delity. His girlfriend was away on business and wouldn't return for a week. Matthew would not see me for another week. He had no business meetings until midafternoon that day. How would Matthew spend the next two hours? Idle minds are the devil's workshop, so the saying goes.

After he left our therapy session Matthew had coffee and eggs at the counter of his favorite diner. The server was an exotic-looking transgender woman, shapely with a touch of sideburns, and his thoughts about her sexual barrier breaking turned him on. No sooner had Matthew ordered his coffee than a beautiful woman in her late twenties took a seat at a nearby stool. Matthew nonchalantly took notice of her every move. When she ordered avocado toast and a glass of Merlot, Matthew thought, *10:45 in the morning, and a glass of Merlot?!? Hmm . . . could this beautiful woman who drinks Merlot with break-fast be my fantasy come true—my random sexual encounter while my girlfriend is out of town?*

I know that such thoughts about having sex with a woman eating breakfast nearby may strike some readers as a bit per-verse, but in my office these musings are exceedingly common among men who tell me everything they are thinking. Matthew tried to make some small talk with her, but his breakfast fantasy woman was far more interested in her Merlot than in Matthew. Despite the lack of engagement, Matthew's fantasies were getting him turned on. He finished his breakfast and left.

What would he do now? Go home and read the paper? Take a walk in the park? Catch up on some work before his meeting? Intending to go home for no good reason—but probably knowing unconsciously that he might go elsewhere—Matthew hopped into a cab. His taxi was getting close to a sex club—a normal-looking brownstone that advertised itself as a spa but instead was where women, for as little as $100 an hour to many hundreds of dollars, would have sex with men. There are many such places masquerading as spas or massage parlors, some for heterosexual men and some for gay men, in Manhattan as well as throughout the country, in red and blue states alike.

Matthew's cab got caught in traffic. Just the excuse he needed. "Why sit in traffic?" Matthew thought. He asked the driver to let him out and leapt from the taxi before he could change his mind. *Should I or shouldn't I?*, he pondered. *I could use a steam bath*, he told himself. But he had no cash.

Matthew went to a nearby ATM to take out enough for the admission fee, telling himself, *I need the cash anyway. Maybe I won't go, but I do need some money*. Then, with a full wallet and his heart pounding, he walked to the brownstone and descended the steps. Matthew slowly undressed for the steam room, and even then he told himself, *This won't be sexual*. He then lay down for his massage session.

Many massage parlors that offer sex also offer legitimate massages. During the massage the masseuse offers the man "extras." The transaction for sex is often done when the masseuse gets to touching near the man's genitals, when he's likely more eager to make a deal. Sometimes the price is negotiated beforehand (pun intended), but usually the man gives a tip based on the services provided, which can vary from manual sex to vaginal or anal intercourse, depending upon the customs of the establishment. Condoms are used rarely for anything other than vaginal or anal sex. At the place Matthew went to, sex was not an add-on but a given. Within minutes of beginning the session the scantily clad masseuse, a sex worker, performed manual and oral sex. As soon as he ejaculated, Matthew was overcome with shame and raced out as quickly as possible.

According to Matthew, at no point was he actually "enjoying" this. He told me that he never experienced anything remotely akin to the lust he felt when he was about to make love to his new girlfriend. Even as the stranger approached his penis, Matthew was desperately *wanting* but not *liking*. On his mission he felt more like the Manchurian candidate than a hot lover, acting almost robotically.

I believe Matthew did not *like* what was happening, even though his behavior demonstrates quite clearly that he *wanted* it to happen; in fact, Matthew did everything to make it happen. Matthew's story is a fairly typical one in my practice. Why do cheaters like him cheat?

First and foremost, Matthew did it because he could. His adultery fulfilled the three A's of misbehavior: it was *accessible*, *affordable*, and *anonymous* sex at a time when Matthew felt he wasn't accountable to anyone.

- accessible: The brothel was right there in front of him.
- affordable: The money was no financial hardship.
- anonymous: Who would find out?

The second reason Matthew cheated is because it fit with his personality or psychological profile. Infidelity can be both an act of arrogant entitlement and self-destructive self-loathing. Matthew had a common personality profile, what psychoanalysts call the narcissistic-masochistic character. His cheating was selfish (narcissistic) but also self-destructive (masochistic). Narcissists seem to have high opinions of themselves, but underneath they harbor very low self-opinions. They use other people to feel better about themselves and don't have very secure attachments. Matthew's narcissism made him devalue the woman who loved him while his self-destructiveness led him to undermine their relationship.

Neuroscience is not yet at the point where I can do much to alter a patient's sexual brain. There is an opiate blocker called Naltrexone, which seems to quiet the reward system, but the impact on sexual obsessions is modest. There are medications that can decrease sexual and general compulsivity—selective serotonin reuptake inhibitors (SSRIs), like Prozac—but no medicine can stop my patients in their tracks. What I *can* do is try to talk some sense into them.

Over a hundred years ago Sigmund Freud wrote that humans contain a desire for love, or Eros, and a desire for destruction, which he called the *death instinct*. Matthew demonstrates both. He had a new partner whom he adored. His job was going better than ever. Yet he sought arousing yet shame-inducing sex that would leave him feeling worthless and lower his self-esteem. He was selfish and arrogant, willing to take chances to get sexual satisfaction, yet he simultaneously solicited his own humiliation. By returning to paid sex, Matthew guaranteed his own heartache. Even if he didn't get caught, he had to live with the dishonesty and indignity.

Next I want to focus on what happened inside his brain that made him do something so hurtful to himself and his partner.

Sex Hormones 101

Unlike your interminable biology class in high school, I promise that my review of your sex hormones will be over in a few paragraphs. Then we'll talk about something your high school teachers never told you: that you can increase your sex hormones by going to a swingers sex club. Let's start at the beginning—with your birth.

Sex hormones create and control our sexual development and appetites. All embryonic fetuses begin female until the sex hormone testosterone, under the influence of the Y chromosome, triggers the development of male characteristics in the fetus. A signal from the pituitary gland, located at the base of the brain, causes the testes in males and the ovaries in females to produce the sexual hormones. During early teenage years both boys and girls produce large amounts of the sex hormones, testosterone and estrogen, to create their physical sexual characteristics and to get the brain to focus on sexual interests.

Men produce ten times more testosterone, which accounts for the development of male features such as facial hair, a deeper voice, and strong lust. Women produce some testosterone as well as estrogen, which is converted to testosterone in their bodies. So although it's more commonly considered a "guy thing," testosterone actually propels the sex drives of both men and women. The hormone increases competitiveness, aggression, and confidence, all of which heighten our desire for and performance during sex. More testosterone means more sexual desire, so some men and women have greater sexual desires solely because they naturally produce more sex hormones.

One physician I spoke with, herself a gynecologist, said that her hormones led her to become a serial cheater. She felt that her philandering was largely due to her polycystic ovary disease, which caused her to make much more testosterone than is usually produced in women. As a result, she said, she wanted sex much more than her normal-testosterone-level husband, so she sought out new sexual adventures. As I will continue to point out over and over again, knowing your biological or psychological predispositions does *not* pardon bad behavior, but it *does* give you insights into how to manage your commitments, needs, and desires.

Keep in mind, for example, that sex hormones wane with age. In men over thirty, testosterone declines roughly 1 to 3 percent each year. In women sex hormone levels drop precipitously after menopause. Given the amount of infidelity that occurs in people's late forties and early fifties, it clearly takes more than just sex hormone levels to lead to cheating.

Just thinking about sex seems to increase testosterone in some people. This creates a positive feedback loop whereby testosterone increases our interest in sex, while our interest in sex, in turn, increases testosterone. Testosterone also turns on other chemicals that make us want sex, including cortisol—one of the chemicals created during high-energy or stressful events—and dopamine, which fuels the brain's reward system. We'll talk in greater detail about dopamine soon.

There is a fascinating study in which social scientists studied the testosterone of forty-four men who attended a heterosexual swingers club in Las Vegas at which the club members participated in group sex. The men who just watched the group sex—in other words, watched but didn't engage in sex—had, on average, an immediate 11 percent increase in their testosterone level. But those males who physically participated in the group sex experienced a whopping 72 percent increase in testosterone. Although the women weren't studied (it is commonly the case that sex studies tend to discriminate against women by not including them in the research), we would expect similar increases among women. The authors noted that their research demonstrates rapid escalation of testosterone in response to sexual stimuli, erotica, and courtship behavior. But the jury is still out on this topic, and other studies have since contradicted their findings. Still, you don't need a scientific test to document what we all know: thinking about sex and getting turned on by sexual stimuli enhances our arousal on a very deep and physiological level.

The Chemicals of Connection

Before we talk about the mess that happens in the brain during adultery, there's one more set of chemicals I need to describe for you. These are what are known as the cuddle chemicals. In 1993 scientists discovered that the roots of mating behavior could be traced to the brain's receptors for oxytocin and vasopressin. Oxytocin, which in Greek means "rapid birth," is the chemical the brain releases right after an orgasm and accounts for the postorgasmic feeling of well-being. It also fosters attachment and maternal bonding. After a mother delivers her infant, oxytocin is released in the mother's body, telling her brain to alert her breasts to get milk flowing for her newborn. Vasopressin, meanwhile, is a hormone that has been associated with blood pressure and kidney function and is now known to also be connected with social bonding. Animal studies have shown that by manipulating brain chemistry, we can actually convert monogamous animals into nonmonogamous animals and vice versa. In the second part of this chapter, when we cover the brain chemicals of bonding in long-term relationships, we'll discuss oxytocin in greater detail.

But first let's talk about what happens when one of my patients goes on a mission to cheat.

What Was Going on Between Matthew's Ears?

Matthew was on a mission to have an orgasm. We know that during his orgasm his brain got flooded with dopamine, similar to what would happen in a brain after a rush of heroin. During orgasm much of the rest of Matthew's brain, including higher functioning, was turned off. Afterward his dopamine levels dropped precipitously, to below their normal level. Depressed levels of dopamine make people sleepy and sometimes even depressed and anxious. Simultaneously the energizing brain chemicals epinephrine and norepinephrine, which were high during sex, dissipate and bring mood and energy down after orgasm.

How do you think Matthew felt after he'd orgasmed and his levels of dopamine, the chemical of "I gotta get it," dissipated? How do you imagine he felt when the chemicals of energy and enthusiasm, epinephrine and norepinephrine, tanked?

Not only did Matthew's dopamine and adrenaline levels drop, but he also experienced the normal postorgasm flood of prolactin, vasopressin, and oxytocin released by the pituitary gland—chemicals that biologically increase our emotional connection to our partner while simultaneously decreasing our sexual arousal.

So how did Matthew feel when the base of his brain released the "cuddle chemicals" and he looked around to find himself not with his loving girlfriend but in a dank room with an unknown, paid sex worker by his side? In a word, he felt like shit. He pledged never to do it again, but as soon as the memories of the day's remorse died and the sirens of desire pointed to this familiar path in his brain, Matthew would find himself traveling down this same road again and again. Until he learned how to break the cycle, Matthew would remain a prisoner of his brain—a brain that *wants* and *craves* but does not *like*.

The Neuroscience of Wanting but Not Liking

On this fateful morning Matthew, like so many of my patients, felt almost robotic, like he was on a preprogrammed mission. He stepped into the spaceship (of lust), pressed the lift-off button, and was gone. Like anyone behaving badly, Matthew could have stopped himself if some barrier stood before him. A police officer, for example, or his girlfriend. Yet without any obvious obstacle, Matthew moved as though under a spell. I'm not saying this to excuse Matthew for choosing to betray his girlfriend—there's no excuse! Instead, I am presenting, for understanding's sake, the credible science indicating how our brains drive us toward rewards—whether it's easy sex or a pint of ice cream late at night after everyone's asleep. If we're unencumbered and undisciplined and the reward seems within easy reach, we—all of us—are hard-pressed to stop ourselves.

Where does this entrancement come from? The reward chemicals of the brain are what cast the spell, and the most important of these is dopamine. Dopamine is the chemical of *wanting* but not necessarily *liking*. Without self-control and the ability to strategically manage our urges, we could all find ourselves driven by dopamine, just like a rat in a cage.

Healthy, normal rats both *like* and *want* salt and sugar. Put a rat in a cage with either, and it will seek out the food and consume it. But remove a rat's dopamine, and it will no longer search for the salt or sugar it enjoys. Without dopamine the rat no longer *wants* the food. In fact, without dopamine the rat may actually starve to death because it no longer experiences *wanting*. Give that same rat an injection of dopamine, however, and the rat once again *wants* sweets and salty and will resume its regular search!

The same goes for sex in humans. For instance, when people take cocaine, which increases dopamine, they may still seek out and have sex, although they find it difficult to orgasm. On cocaine humans keep going at sex like the Energizer bunny until physical exhaustion sets in. Dopamine, the chemical of desire, or *wanting*, makes my patients like Matthew go on their mission, even if they say they don't actually *like* where the mission leads them—even if they know it's bad for them and their relationships.

In fact, Matthew's drive, which seemed beyond his comprehension, can be traced to a tiny part of his brain, no bigger than the size of a pinhead, called the *dorsal ventral pallidum*. The ventral pallidum is involved in many aspects of behavior, from lust to prosocial yearnings such as altruism. The dorsal ventral pallidum is where the reward and motivation centers converge and are conducted throughout the brain. Scientists call this the hedonic hotspot for pleasure-inducing thoughts and behaviors, and it also houses the brain receptors that may partly account for both monogamy and infidelity in animals.

The Animal Model for the Neuroscience of Monogamy and Nonmonogamy

Although few mammals stay together after sex to rear their offspring, and most venture off to have sex with other animals throughout their lives, there is one type of rodent, a particular species of vole, that was thought to be faithful for life. These rodents are especially interesting because they are nearly identical to another breed of voles that don't stay together after procreation. The monogamous voles live in the prairie (*Microtus ochrogaster*), and the nonmonogamous live in the meadow (*Microtus montanus*). Biologically speaking, these two types of voles are almost identical genetically. The single-great exception is a difference in their brain receptors that exist on their tiny, pinpoint-sized ventral pallidum and the associated nucleus accumbens.

The prairie voles are among the estimated 3 to 5 percent of mammals who appear to stay mated forever. (As we'll discuss later, even the 10 to 20 percent of prairie voles who do stray still remain socially bonded to their mates and offspring.) Most prairie vole males protect their mates and attack competitors, while partners rear their young together, living as a unit, and their social pups long to be with their parents. In fact, prairie vole pups let out a cry when left alone too early.

Meadow voles, however, are relative loners. They remain isolated and independent, and they mate freely. Male and female meadow voles abandon their offspring at an early age, and their pups take it in stride. The meadow voles are not monogamous at all. They form few social bonds. They copulate and leave.

The difference between these two groups of animals is found in the brain receptors for the two neurotransmitters, vasopressin and oxytocin, that promote the behaviors of social bonding and attachment. As evolution would have it, the more monogamous prairie voles have a higher density of these receptors, which means they more readily process the "cuddle" brain chemicals that promote bonding.

Turning the Philandering into the Faithful

With scientific manipulation researchers have been able to adjust the brain chemicals in these rodents, successfully turning monogamous voles into nonmonogamous voles and vice versa. Hence, when the nonmonogamous meadow voles are dosed with oxytocin and vasopressin, they become monogamous.

In the wild, prairie voles need to spend at least sixteen to twenty hours with multiple bouts of mating before they develop a social bond that lasts a lifetime. In the lab, however, if researchers give them vasopressin or oxytocin, they can induce this social bonding within six hours, with no mating at all. The brain-chemical infusion, along with some casual hanging out, is enough to bond these voles for life. Strong stuff!

Love Is the Drug

"The addiction centers of our brain that send dopamine surging did not evolve to foster addictions to drugs like cocaine or heroin. [Instead] those centers evolved to motivate behaviors that are important for our survival and reproduction," writes Dr. Larry Young, director of the Center for Translational Social Neuroscience at Emory University. Dr. Young has been studying social and sexual bonding for the past twenty-two years, and according to him, humans developed vulnerabilities to addiction so we would become addicted to our babies!

Makes sense, doesn't it? In order to entice a mother to risk her own life to give birth to and take care of her babies, the mammalian brain needed to have the social bonding system linked to the brain's reward center. All mammal species, from rats to humans, have this oxytocin-driven maternal bond. Scientists like Dr. Young think the same brain circuits that get directed toward caring for one's young also get directed toward other individuals, including sexual partners. Oxytocin helps the deep reward centers of our brain to receive and encode the neural information related to one's partner, such as their face, smell, and voice. And because these encodings are also associated with rewards—meaning dopamine—scientists think the neural encoding of a partner gets hardwired into the reward system so that the partner becomes *inherently* rewarding.

A loving attachment connection is like heroin to us. Once we have it, we don't want to give it up. And if it gets taken away, our brains go into love withdrawal. Dr. Young found that the adrenals of voles separated from their partners get larger, and they then produce more stress hormones. The loss of a partner brings about signs of depression. "They actually go through withdrawal of oxytocin due to the lack of the partner being around," explained Dr. Young. "I think that is a mechanism that keeps relationships together for a long period of time. We become dependent on each other."

Human Studies

In 2008 Swedish researchers, including Dr. Hasse Walum, studied 552 couples and found that, like in the voles, there are genetic variations that may be related to fidelity. They later hypothesized that social bonding in men may correspond with the density in a specific region of the brain containing vasopressin receptors. Studies have shown that men with a certain receptor gene makeup had twice as many marital crises. This could indicate that abnormalities in the genes that control vasopressin production may actually create problems with sustaining long-term relationships. Although researchers did not study whether there were more episodes of philandering among these men, the authors did examine several factors, including: marital happiness, discovering a link between vasopressin receptor gene abnormalities and social skills; marital satisfaction as confirmed independently by their partners; the men's tendency to get married and stay married; and numbers of crises in the relationship. Tolstoy once wrote that all happy families are said to be alike and all unhappy families are different or "unhappy in their own way." Maybe. Or maybe all unhappy families simply have very similar DNA!

In 2012 the same group of researchers published data on women. They found a very similar relationship between bonding and marital discord and oxytocin receptor genes. In addition, the researchers noted that there was a correlation between the oxytocin receptor gene and poor social bonding in childhood.

Since the initial groundbreaking research in 2008, lead researcher Dr. Walum has teamed up with Dr. Young to explore more directly what humans and voles have in common when it comes to social bonding. Most surprising and extraordinary for Dr. Walum and his team are the similarities they discovered between these structures in both humans and voles. According to their research, what we call love and devotion is a function of evolution hijacking brain systems that were already in place for territoriality and maternal behavior in all animals. Male animals, say scientists, are particularly territorial (territoriality is the evolutionary antecedent of human jealousy). That is partly a result of the vasopressin gene acting in the ventral pallidum. Both female and male animals have the inherent desire to parent and take care of their young, and that is partly a result of the oxytocin genes acting in the nucleus accumbens.

Evolution developed humans who will remain together, at least long enough to raise some viable offspring. As such, these scientists believe that hundreds of thousands of years ago evolution utilized the preexisting animal systems for territoriality and offspring-rearing behavior to create humans who are monogamous . . . or at least humans who aspire to be monogamous. More *monogamish* than monogamous.

The Course of Love

Scientists who study relationships believe that the relatively short first phase of "being in love" usually lasts around six months and evolves into a longer phase of "passionate love," which can last for several years, followed then by the third phase of a relationship: companion love, which is akin to very close friendships. Oxytocin has been shown in humans to play a substantial role in the process of establishing a pair bond in the first stage of romantic love.

Israeli researchers studied oxytocin levels in sixty couples three months after the initiation of their romantic relationship and compared them with forty-three nonattached singles. They found that levels of oxytocin in the blood predicted whether the new lovers would still be romantically involved six months later. Couples with higher oxytocin levels at the initial period of romantic attachment were more likely to stay together. These findings suggest that oxytocin in the first months of romantic love may help predict whether a relationship will last.

In another study German researchers gave twenty men either oxytocin or a placebo and then showed them pictures of their partners and either another woman that people rated to be equally attractive or a female friend. They then asked the men to rate the attractiveness of the people in those pictures. The men who received a dose of synthetic oxytocin rated their partner as being more attractive, while those who received the placebo did not. Oxytocin made the men view their partners as being more attractive but did *not* make the men view other women as more attractive. The men were shown the photographs while undergoing brain scans, which allowed researchers to see what parts of the brain were activated when they were given oxytocin, saw pictures of their partners, and found their mates more attractive. The nucleus accumbens, the same reward center area studied in the vole research, was the area that "lit up."

In a related study Drs. Bianca Acevedo, Helen Fisher, and Lucy Brown measured blood activity in the brain as a means of identifying where romantic thoughts seem to reside. The study first showed a subject inside a brain scanner a photo of the person they were in love with, then distracted them with a difficult math problem to "wash" the brain of further romantic thoughts, and finally showed a neutral photo for which the subject had no discernible emotion. When the subjects were feeling romantic love, these researchers found the highest levels of brain activation in the *ventral tegmental area* of the brainstem, which is known to be the brain's dopamine "factory" and therefore is a key area for pleasure, rewards, and sex. In other research Dr. Fisher has also found that when people lose a partner, their brains look similar to those of drug addicts suffering withdrawal.

✗ ✗ ✗

To recap, Matthew got in trouble when he impulsively searched for sexual gratification. His lust, as we've discussed, originated in the most primitive parts of his brain, driven by the brain chemicals testosterone, dopamine, epinephrine, oxytocin, and vasopressin. Swept up by his turned-on state, he allowed himself to be controlled by the rewards center, located in the middle of the brain. Meanwhile his frontal lobes underwent chemical changes that helped them go along for the ride and support the rewards center's mission.

Psychologically speaking, meanwhile, when Matthew allowed lust to overtake him, he was being driven by his selfishness, self-destructiveness, and fears of being alone when his girlfriend was out of town. We have also seen that faithfulness or fidelity can be encoded in our genes and regulated by our brain chemicals. We have excellent animal models and human studies to prove that brain chemistry counts. In this chapter I've tried to make clear that impulsive lust, infatuation, love, and bonding, along with the sadness of losing a loved one, are all too human as well as also chemically driven.

You can't cheat and, when caught, tell your spouse, "My genes made me do it" or "Blame evolution." When it comes to our behavior choices, our values and culture, our parents, and our experiences influence us the most. But although the roles of culture and psychology are of paramount importance, the influence of biology should not to be ignored. If we ignore the role of brain chemistry in the actions we do and don't take, we might be undone by these unseen forces. To paraphrase James Baldwin's quote from the Introduction, you can't fix what you don't understand.

part two

the taste for new sex

Orgies, threesomes, cybersex, BDSM, novelty—these desires open up worlds of anticipation, lust, and fantasy. And they are often the longings that propel us toward infidelity. In this section we'll talk about the cravings that push and pull us to look outside our primary relationship for love and sex. We'll talk about how my patients address those desires in a long-standing relationship. We will distinguish between emotional affairs and physical affairs as well as discussing the differences between emotional and sexual infidelities. I will explain, based on the research, how men and women may differ in what they are looking for in an affair. Finally, in what I think is the most important part of this section, we will learn from the experiences of actual people about how to heal when conflicting desires threaten to tear apart our most important love relationships.

chapter 4

Cyber relationships and America's obsession with porn

M any men (and some women) develop sexual affairs online, whereas many women (and some men) develop emotional affairs. In this chapter I will address the ways in which the internet enables many types of cyber-sexual relationships. I'll also discuss how America's interest in porn sometimes rises to the level of a competing sexual interest, causing almost as much damage as an affair. In the following chapter I will delve into the murky and controversial topic of emotional affairs, which can take place both on- and offline.

The Newest Tool for the Cheater

Most of us want sex, love, and attachment, yet searching for love and then sabotaging it with restless wandering seems to be part of the human condition. We seem to be programmed to find dissatisfaction with our mates, undermining the very partnerships designed to provide us with exactly what we're seeking. Sexual and romantic connections can bring us to the highest planes of human existence, something akin to a religious or spiritual experience. We want to believe in fidelity, and most of us sign up for a monogamous partnership. Yet inevitably many of us become disenchanted with our long-term partners at some point, at least for a time. When we first meet our love, all their failings are tolerable. Yet our desire for one partner can wane after even a few months of a relationship, not to mention decades of boredom, bills, burdens, defeats, and disappointments. After years of togetherness some of our partner's traits can perturb us terribly.

Research confirms that the initial rush of infatuation with your partner typically lasts for the first six months. After the infatuation wears off, the feeling of being in love can last for a few years. Although over time many of us lose the intense feeling of being in love with our partner, we rarely lose our *desire* to be in love and lust. As such, we all have the potential to get lost in fantasy, intrigue, love, and sex. This creates fertile ground for infidelity. No longer confined to "cheaters" bars or secret rendezvous during business trips, infidelity is committed by everyday people of all stripes online.

The internet has made infidelity a key social issue of the twenty-first century, offering a technological playground for philanderers. Technology is turning previously out-of-reach fantasies into instant opportunities. In fact, all of my unfaithful patients have used the internet to procure and facilitate opportunities with new lovers.

Cheaters, Beware!

Seemingly anonymous contacts over digital networks have made discovering infidelity much easier. Divorce lawyers write that cell phones have become a major way that a cheating spouse is revealed. My clinical experience bears this out. The transgressions of nearly all my philandering patients are most often revealed when a spouse finds an email or text that is just the tip of the iceberg.

Even without reading your texts or emails, a spouse can simply search your browser history—from tracking your online porn use to spying on your googled questions about sex and affairs—to see what you're thinking or yearning for. A cell phone may feel anonymous and impenetrable, but in my experience cheating spouses don't keep their secrets for long. A suspicious partner will ultimately demand the passwords. Your device retains a record that is a window into your unconscious and is not deleted by simply clearing your history.

Wronged Spouses, Be Warned!

If you're the cheated-upon spouse, the record of your unfaithful partner will quite likely drive you into a compulsive frenzy of wanting to read all the sordid details. You will search for evidence that you can trust them and that they still love you or to see how many times they lied. Either way, as an aggrieved spouse, you may find yourself drawn to painfully scrutinizing every word of the wanderings of your cheating partner's mind on their cell phone, tablet, and laptop.

As we'll discuss in more detail later, this tendency, called *pain shopping,* is not helpful. The information you find on this type of hunt will likely haunt you, bringing very little benefit and great cost. We'll also discuss better ways of dealing with feelings of betrayal than going into surveillance mode on your spouse.

The Internet: Dopamine Multiplier

One of the first digital pager services, called Blackberries, were known as "crackberries" as a tongue-in-check reference to how they were supposedly as addictive as crack. Today the internet, whether accessed by smartphone, tablet, or computer, creates so much instant gratification and dopamine release that it would be apt to call it a magnifier of the dopamine reward centers. Even without googling anything related to sex, the internet in and of itself offers instant gratification and can consume many waking hours. When we combine the instant gratification of the internet's inherent compulsion loop with the innate rewards of sex, it's clear why the combination of sex and internet is so potent—a dopamine multiplier.

Researchers estimate that somewhere between 4 and 15 percent of the internet's use is for porn, with 10 percent being the number upon which academics tend to agree. For better or worse, the United States is the number-one consumer of internet porn. Internet technology has revolutionized the ease of cheating and redefined extramarital encounters.

When it comes to the use of the internet for purely sexual contact, online porn is the most common example. Aside from porn, the internet is commonly used for sending photos or texts to an online partner. Accessed through direct search—or via one of the many pop-up windows that appear during porn watching to redirect viewers to web cams, encounters, or paid sexual contact with an actual woman whom they can watch masturbate online in real time—these sites offer the possibility of more one-on-one contact. Such interactions often involve engagement in a group chat followed by a sidebar conversation, which can involve web cams, Skype, or FaceTime show-and-tell of genitals and masturbation.

No longer do prostitutes need to hang out on street corners or rely on pimps to do business; instead, today's sex workers can simply post on sites like Craigslist, Backpage, or Eros to advertise their wares. As has happened for so many other commodities, web-based technologies have made it easy to shop for sex. Clients can specify more precisely the type of prostitute they wish to hire and can even negotiate with some civility the type of sexual encounter they're seeking. Today prostitution is not only easier and quicker but also safer for the sex worker. The sex worker's and sex seeker's vetting processes can be longer and more thorough. The sex worker can even google their "john" and get a credit card and ID upfront, while the sex seeker can read online reviews (like choosing a restaurant based on patron recommendations). Research has also shown that the transmission of sexually transmitted disease such as HIV has decreased with transactions originating through the internet instead of the street corner.

Most real-life, digitally influenced encounters involve an erotic mixture of online and offline encounters that activate the romance, intrigue, and desire centers in our brains. Whether we are talking about paid sex or falling in love with an old flame, the bulk of *virtual affairs* are internet-enabled, real-life rendezvous in which you contact someone online—through social media or an advertised site—and develop a quick and intense sexual and/or romantic interest in them that leads to crossing what's called the *flesh line* by having an in-person physical encounter.

Sometimes the order gets switched, like when you meet someone in person, for instance, at a party or a professional meeting, and then the relationship takes a romantic and/or sexual direction through virtual communication. Although affair partners may live hundreds or thousands of miles away, by virtue of the internet, social media, text, and web-cam technologies a relationship can move forward at the pace of Wifi, with the instant gratification of the internet abetted by the intensity of the turned-on brain.

When Is Porn a Problem, and When Does It Count as Infidelity?

Let's return to the issue of porn. A survey of 15,246 US-based respondents found that 75 percent of men and 41 percent of women had intentionally viewed or downloaded porn. For an estimated 98 percent of users internet porn is neither a compulsion nor considered by most spouses to be an act of infidelity. For most men and women who use porn, watching is just a pastime; they can take it or leave it. Surveys in the United States and Europe indicate that between 1.5 and 8.2 percent of the population qualify as problematic internet users, defined as having "excessive or poorly controlled preoccupations, urges, or behaviors regarding computer use and internet access that lead to impairment or distress."

There is some data that porn causes problems with arousal, attraction, and sexual performance. Women have reported that porn watching lowered their own body image, made them feel their partner was critical of their body, increased pressure to perform acts seen in porn, and led to less actual sex. Men, meanwhile, reported being more critical of their partners' bodies and less interested in actual sex. However, I've also seen through my practice that porn can do the opposite as well: increasing desire, teaching new techniques, and maybe even providing new ways for couples to get turned on together.

Trouble arises when porn use, instead of enhancing sex, replaces one's interest in one's partner or interferes with home and work obligations. And even if time isn't the issue, what if the pornographic material viewed is *too* graphic, violent, or otherwise offensive? At what point does porn become the new affair partner? Who makes these determinations? You, your spouse, the police, religious leaders, your doctors? And if it's your doctor, which doctor, as their opinions may vary as much as anybody's?

In his study of 267 men and women with compulsive sexual problems, Dr. Aviv Weinstein, the senior coauthor of a chapter in my textbook on internet addiction, found that online sexual activity, including porn consumption, threatened "the economic, emotional, and relational stability of marriages and families" and was "significantly associated with decreased marital sexual satisfaction and sexual intimacy." Weissman found that both men and women perceived internet-based sexual activity to be as threatening to a marriage as offline infidelity.

Another study, conducted through surveying one hundred women whose partners watched porn, showed that nearly a third of the women felt "moderate to high levels of distress about their partner's use of such material." Concerns included fears that their partners were picturing porn stars during sex with them and feeling that their partners were less trustworthy when they kept porn use a secret, which many did even when the women didn't object to it.

The Wide World of Porn

In their 2016 annual review of users' viewing habits, Pornhub reported nearly ninety-two billion video views on their site that year. "That's 12.5 videos viewed for every person on earth," the report boasted. For its part, the United States not only topped out Pornhub's per capita page views at 221 but also remained the number-one porn producer.

Peak porn-watching hours (dubbed *fappy hour*) fell between 11 P.M. and 1:00 A.M., and "lesbian" was the site's most popular search term overall, followed by "stepmom," "MILF" (moms-I'd-like-to-f###), "teen," "stepsister," and "mom." Incest terms gained popularity in 2016. California accounted for the largest number of "lesbian" searches, whereas people in Nebraska, Arkansas, Tennessee, and Vermont did the most searching for "cartoon" porn, and "ebony" topped the charts in Mississippi, Louisiana, Georgia, and Delaware. Viewers in Wyoming, Montana, Minnesota, Ohio, and Maine sought out the most "stepsister" content, and Alaska, Washington, Kentucky, and New Hampshire gave "stepmom" top billing.

Not only do porn choices reflect forbidden fruit, but porn can also perpetuate male and female stereotypes and undermine good sex in real life. According to the 2017 scientific paper in the *Journal of Sex Research*, "representations of male and female orgasm in mainstream pornography may serve to perpetuate unrealistic beliefs and expectations in relation to female orgasm and male sexual performance."

There's nothing wrong with consenting sex, of course. But it's worth considering how the barrage of intense novel scenes available online might make real sex with a real partner seem boring. Add to that the fact that the average first exposure to porn occurs when an adolescent's brain is still forming (usually by age eleven), and you begin to sense how we may be damaging our minds and hurting ourselves as well as our long-term relationships.

Porn and Cybersex Can Put Your Brain into "Flow"

To comprehend the spaceship feeling that affects many of my patients, it helps to understand the science behind the trance that internet porn can throw some of us into—what researchers have come to call *flow*. Typically described as peak moments of complete absorption and engagement, flow is a state commonly found among professional athletes active in their sport. But the notion of flow can also apply in the realm of sexual desire.

In the 1970s psychologist Mihaly Csikszentmihalyi coined the term *flow* to describe a state of consciousness in which the person is so consumed and engaged that time evaporates and the outside world fades into the background, leaving people so involved in their activity that little else seems to matter to the brain. Later scientists sought to identify the actual transformations in the brain that caused this feeling of flow. Neuroscientist Mihaly Csikszentmihalyi was among those who helped discover the radical change in normal brain function that results in heightened attention, slower conscious processing, and faster, more efficient processing of the subconscious system.

Flow can also be thought of as what you feel when you're lost in a daydream. Daydreams are not actual dreams, of course—you're not sleeping. None of the loss of consciousness or rapid eye movements (REM) that occur when you sleep and dream are present while awake. But the brain activity during this daydream state differs from normal, reality-based thought. Seen on an EEG, electrical activity of the brain is altered when you are immersed in a daydream. In this daydream/flow state the frontal lobes' executive functions—essential to our ability to

Anthony's story: Preoccupied with porn

This literal deceleration of higher cognitive functioning was the force at play for my patient Anthony, who found himself lost in sexual daydreams and touching himself even while at work.

All my patients are driven by fantasy, but the one most held captive by his mind is Anthony. When he first came to me for treatment, he told me he had a "major problem with porn." In addition to his vivid imagination that easily led him into a state of sexual daydream, he also had a habit of watching one to three hours of porn per day, oftentimes at work. He loved his wife deeply, and they still had great sex. When Anthony told his wife some of the details about his porn obsession, she was deeply offended and angry and, in response, sought nonstop sex with him in an effort to keep him from the habit. But none of that curbed his obsession.

It was more than clear to Anthony, his wife, and his group therapy mates—not to mention me, his psychiatrist—that porn, for Anthony, had definitely reached the point of trouble. Anthony's problem had risen to an addiction when it began competing with and undermining his relationship with his wife. In treatment Anthony was very honest with himself. Through talk therapy he began to gain new insights into the inner workings of his brain so he could better anticipate and manage the triggers that might lead him back down the sexual daydream path that would hijack higher brain functioning. One step he

plan, make decisions, form judgments, assess risk, and formulate insight—essentially get turned off.

Beyond Porn: Online Sexual Play Is Here to Stay

Porn aside, social media and other sites have made it relatively easy to develop a romantic or erotic attachment to another took toward healing was to "deporn" all his computers. Eventually this helped Anthony rein in his habit.

But stressful circumstances posed perpetual challenges. In the six months that followed the death of his brother, Anthony was also struggling with problems with his children. The strain made his escapes into porn and fantasy look ever so attractive, and he shared his dismay with the other men in our group therapy sessions. Anthony explained that his brother had left him two laptops, and because they were not blocked, he'd started looking at porn on them. "It upset me. I felt so ridiculous."

"Stress pushes us to act out," Bob replied, trying to offer reassurance. "You're asking for yourself to be hardwired differently." Then I jumped in to explain the neurological reality behind how difficult it is for people like Anthony and Bob to resist the pull of sexual escape. When they're stimulated by what they see, what they hear, what they smell, the visual brain centers (occipital lobes) team up with the brain's reward centers (the limbic system), while the brain's reasoning centers (frontal lobes) are left trying to talk sense. When the brain has memorized the pathways to porn, the effect is overwhelming. The best remedy is for these men to extricate themselves from the trigger. And that's exactly what Anthony did. He later explained to the group that he took a sledgehammer to his brother's laptops, destroying them one by one. The act reflected a desire to destroy a part of himself that he just couldn't shake but instead would need to learn to cope with.

person without any physical contact as well as paving the way for easy offline physical connections. Tinder, Match, Ashley Madison—each of these web-based services offers its own sexual and romantic possibilities for cheaters. The internet has revolutionized porn, prostitution, hooking up, and even falling in love.

The internet permits the easy kindling of not only instant sexual gratification but also instant intimacy. For people feeling a diminished connection in their primary relationships, new technologies have made it easier to cultivate and maintain a virtual affair—a secret relationship that feels more important, erotic, or intimate than the relationship with one's real-life partner. (In the next chapter we'll have more to say about online affairs that are ostensibly platonic—so called emotional affairs. So if you want to think ahead to Chapter 5, ask yourself: *Are emotional affairs cheating?*)

Unlike most affairs, online sex play often begins in the home, right under your own roof. Its primary tools are the phone, tablet, or computer, and eliminating these enablers is not usually an option. As such, these devices can become a philanderer's ever-present temptation as well as an ever-present reminder to a betrayed spouse of their partner's transgressions. The days of hiding—or discovering—receipts from dinners or hotel stays have been replaced. Today's philanderer can be sharing a meal with their spouse while sexting with someone else.

Part of the trouble comes from the way technology allows participants to take on whatever identity they choose, at least for a time. As Katherine Hertlein, PhD, an associate professor at the University of Nevada in Las Vegas, writes in an article for the American Psychological Association, "You don't have to be this constrained person you think you should be. Your primary partner will never be able to compare with the fantasy partner. They will never win."

The instant intimacy fostered by new technologies, the difficulties of maintaining committed relationships, and the impulsive nature of desire combined with our longings for sexual and personal connections create a volatile mix. It's instant gratification! But which forays qualify as cheating? I say this is a tough call. Of course, you can do what most people do—hide, lie, and ignore your own sex-charged behaviors and those of your spouse. Or, if you're willing to consider other possibilities, read on.

Digital Relationships with Real People

What we call a *virtual affair* is essentially a sexual relationship initiated and maintained online. Many experts have written about these relationships that start off as, say, a simple exchange or an innocent email and then develop into full-fledged sex over the airwaves. "Cybersex involves online users swapping texts based on sexual fantasies," addiction expert Dr. Mark Griffiths explains. "Online chat rooms provide opportunities for online social gatherings to occur at the push of a button without even having to move from your desk . . . the easiest, most disinhibiting and most accessible way to meet potential new partners."

Internet Opportunists

When I asked my men's therapy group "How much does the reason you're here have to do with the fact that the internet exists?" the men were unanimous. Most of them had suffered such negative consequences from connections they'd made online that they now dedicated one evening each week to working to overcome the temptation. As Anthony put it, regardless of their social status and income, by virtue of the internet "we have as much opportunity as rock stars. We're living

Seeking arrangements

Charlie was always the good boy in his Catholic family, a hard worker, honest, and earnest. Routinely rejected by attractive girls, Charlie was out of touch with his sexuality and plagued by guilt about his sexual desires and masturbation habit. When his academic success in high school landed him acceptance to an Ivy League university, he looked forward to new possibilities. He saw his first porn movie at a bachelor party and became captivated by the idea of anal sex. "I was dumbfounded. I didn't know that was even possible." *What else was possible?* he wondered.

Upon graduation Charlie's business career took off, and within a decade he was making more money than he'd ever dreamt of. Meanwhile he continued to learn about sex that he'd never dreamt of as well. Before long he married a kind and beautiful woman, his soul mate who, without a doubt, he explained, was the best woman he could ever hope to have as a life partner and mother of his children.

Still, within a year after his wedding Charlie began cheating with a woman he met at Tiffany's while purchasing an expensive gift for his new wife. She turned him on, offering "forbidden" sexual experiences like anal sex, tying her up, and nearly choking her during intercourse. She was just the first of many people with whom Charlie cheated.

Some fifteen years later Charlie ended up in my office after becoming consumed with a site called SeekingArrangements.com,

like baseball players, actors, and athletes." He quickly added that these opportunities destroyed marriages: "You know, celebrities' marriages never last."

Kevin explained it this way: "You see, we have the opportunity, and we're in that position because of the internet. It's hard to remain faithful." Bob, the group's elder statesman who which advertises itself as "Home to over 5 Million Sugar Babies, Sugar Daddies, & Sugar Mommas." The site's founder writes, "Every successful relationship is an arrangement between two parties. In business, partners sign business agreements that outline their objectives and expectations. Likewise, romantic relationships can only work if two people agree on what they expect, and what they can give and receive from each other."

To the businessman in Charlie this made perfect sense. He could have his cake (in this case, a girlfriend) and eat it too (keep his family together and maintain the appearance of stability and respectability). For a few thousand a month per girlfriend, Charlie could bed a college student (or two) as his schedule permitted. With the women on his payroll, he could do all the things that weren't part of his sexual repertoire with his wife.

And yet his dalliances—compulsive and ultimately unsatisfying—were also causing him trouble. It took months of intensive treatment for him to recognize that he could not, in fact, both have his cake and eat it without destroying what was fundamentally most important to him: his family. He needed to understand that he had been seeking not just sex but the chance to seize power over young, attractive women who offered themselves up to him for a fee. He needed to understand that his pursuit of younger women who made him feel "vital and virile" was an attempt to ease his fears about growing old. (We'll pick up Charlie's story again a little later.)

had grown up long before the internet, elaborated. "You can push it now. People had so little opportunity before. We have such good access."

To come full cycle, the spouses of all the men in this group had discovered their husbands' philandering by the trails they'd left in their email and texts. The internet both enabled their cheating with a sense of omnipotence and subsequently led the men to wind up caught with their hands in the cookie jar. Even as the internet provides the illusion of anonymity and being erasable, in truth your browser provides an indelible record of your actions.

The illusion of anonymity granted by digital communications is one significant draw—users can feel free to try on different personas, experiment with different sexual identities, and revel in escapist fantasies. As we've discussed earlier, social scientists seeking to explain the social mechanics of addiction created a trifecta of conditions they coined the *triple-A engine*, which includes *access*, *affordability*, and *anonymity*. Subsequently, a researcher named Dr. Kimberly Young devised a model to account for the intensity and attractiveness of online technology for overindulging in sexual material in particular. She dubbed it the *ACE* model, for *anonymity*, *convenience*, and *escape*. Simply put, accessing sex, pixelated or otherwise, through the internet is effortless, cheap, and easy to get away with. The ready availability allows users to act impulsively online and, perhaps most importantly, get lost in another world or worlds—transported to a different headspace.

Cyber Affair Warning Signs

Experts say that the first signs of a virtual affair could include a partner whose personality has changed. They might exhibit a change in sleeping habits, suddenly demand privacy, ignore other responsibilities, and seem to be lying, less interested in sex, or less invested in their primary relationship. Often the unsuspecting spouse may actually know the affair partner, and then, after the friendship evolves into romance, the cheating spouse begins to withhold data or downplay the relationship. Before long, as strong feelings swell, people often stop mentioning the other person at all. Of course other telltale signs could include hiding devices, changing passwords, and an awful lot of denial.

Some might charge that anyone's pursuit of escape from their marital difficulties through online channels demonstrates a lack of commitment to their relationship. If someone is so devoted to porn and outside stimulation or is determined to find a fling on Facebook, perhaps they should be divorced. But it's important to consider the power that internet access provides as a window for opportunity, where anonymity, affordability, and access could rock the best of relationships. No matter how they are accessed, it's important to keep in mind that affairs of the heart and journeys of sexual desire overtake the reward centers of the brain. New sex and love clouds or subverts the frontal lobes' decision-making abilities, and these biological, evolutionarily adaptive processes are hard to surmount.

chapter 5

The emotional affair

C an men and women be just friends? Although most people agree that sex outside of a monogamous marriage qualifies as an affair, the rules and expectations surrounding emotional affairs are not so clear-cut. When does an intimate, nonsexual relationship with someone other than a spouse qualify as infidelity? And how often do these sorts of relationships occur? Can't people who might otherwise consider each other as potential mates choose to be *just* friends?

I'm old enough to recall the 1989 movie *When Harry Met Sally*. Two acquaintances from college, played by Billy Crystal (Harry) and Meg Ryan (Sally), run into each other years later and Harry says, "What I'm saying is—and this is not a come-on in any way, shape, or form—is that men and women can't be friends because the sex part always gets in the way." Sally finds that offensive and calls him a caveman: "You are a human affront to all women." They part ways and meet again five years later, when they are both in committed relationships. They decide to give friendship a try and quickly become best buddies. They vent and complain to each other about problems in their respective romantic relationships until finally—you guessed it—they end up in bed together, then married three months later.

When the film came out I was just starting my psych residency. I got a call from the *Today Show*, which was looking to find a psychiatrist who studied sex and could answer the question: *Can men and women truly be friends?* Like Sally in the movie, I found the very question offensive. Men have more on their minds than just sex! We aren't cavemen! My gay and lesbian friends had many sexually appealing same-gender friends who remained *just* friends. I saw the question as so old-fashioned, so insulting to any liberated and reasonable person's intelligence, that I refused to go on the show.

Twenty-five years later I told this story to my men's group, asking for their thoughts. "Can men and women be best friends and nothing more?"

Anthony was quick to respond. "We are compelled, as men, to turn everything into a sex event."

Bob said, "You know the joke, 'Why did God give women vaginas? So men will talk to them.'"

The group laughed, but I wanted to scream at them, as it was that objectification of women that had led them to needing treatment in my office.

"I've never had a friend who's a woman," said Kevin.

Anthony jumped in and said, "I do, but I need to stay away from her 'cause I am just wanting to—"

I interrupted. "Come on, guys, you can be friends with a woman, can't you?" incredulous at their mentality.

But Pete, a religious man, fired back defensively, "Observant men have said 'no.' Learned men and pious religious scholars have studied this and arrived at the same conclusion as us—that men and women cannot be—"

"I apologize," I interrupted. "I'm not feeling superior, and I completely understand what you're saying."

Then Roger asked me, "So what do *you* think? Can *you* be best friends with a woman?" For the most part, I am usually very circumspect and reveal little about myself to my patients, often reverting to the usual therapeutic stance of throwing the question back at them with a practiced reply of "What do *you* think?" But in group there's an equality among all members, even me, and not answering when everyone else is baring their soul seems wrong. So I confessed. "I have been very close and remain very close to many wonderful, attractive, and available women. And it is nothing more than friendship. So yes, I feel I can and should be close friends with women."

But even as the words left my mouth, I realized that I wasn't telling the complete truth, that sexual tension was an element in some of my relationships with women. In fact, it was the glue that kept two of my friendships with women together. So, twenty-five years later, I realized that despite me turning my nose up at the idea, the *Today Show* indeed had a point! Of course, men and women could be best friends. But when both people are attracted to each other, what initially passes for friendship can actually be unspoken desire and a connection that could wind up undermining a primary relationship—in other words, the seeds of an emotional affair.

Why porn is addictive

Anonymity

Surely anyone who's spent any time communicating via email, text, or social media has experienced how easy it is for people to reveal themselves much faster than might otherwise occur during in-person encounters. The phenomenon is not unlike the experience of meeting someone on a plane—only online you don't need to see someone's face, dress up, or worry about how you smell. Instead, you're basically lost in your imaginings, your hopes, and your desires—lost in the well of your own subconscious and unconscious.

People have the illusion of anonymity on the internet, affording them a greater sense of control over how they present themselves. That anonymity, that comfort to share freely, leads to an accelerated intimacy. Online—at least without a web cam involved—it's impossible to see the visual signs of insincerity, judgment, or disapproval that would be a natural part of interactions in person.

Convenience

The convenience of online interaction goes without saying. Between computers, smartphones, and tablets, whole worlds of sexual content lie in wait just a keystroke or finger swipe away. And the omnipresence of these devices can pose serious challenges for those seeking to avoid easy access to their compulsive behaviors. Built into this element are the factors of both accessibility and acceptability of "cruising" online.

Readers of a certain age will remember a time when newspaper classified sections posted "lonely hearts" listings, when the main pick-up spots were bars, and when adult bookstores, movie houses, and novelty shops were where people (mostly men) went to see porn. Now not only are these opportunities available in the privacy of your

continues

own home, but many sites—even those specifically geared toward infidelity (like Ashley Madison, which purportedly has signed up fifty-seven million members)—have reached a state of social acceptability. And given the long work hours that many Americans maintain, the convenience of digital technologies for addressing sexual desires is crucial.

Escape

In this context the notion of escape means seeking experiences that help you leave real life behind in pursuit of activities that elevate your mood. As Dr. Kimberly Young explains, "Cyber affairs and cyber sexual encounters are typically a symptom of an underlying problem that existed in the marriage." As such, the bonds established with people through technology can offer new sources of "excitement, romance, and passion that may be missing in a current relationship." Some people use cyber affairs as an easy escape from the real issues plaguing their relationships rather than delving into the hard work of reconciliation. Instead, cyber affairs serve as an outlet for unexpressed emotions as well as a coping mechanism for dealing with hurt feelings arising in the primary relationship.

In addition to the trifecta of *anonymity, convenience,* and *escape,* other addiction concepts provide helpful models for understanding exactly how some people can get so lost on the internet. The key, relevant aspects of addiction are *tolerance* and *withdrawal.*

Tolerance

A psychological and physiological construct, *tolerance* means that the brain requires more and more of a stimulus to have the same effect. When it comes to sex that means that what turns us on today may do less for us tomorrow. To better grasp the concept, consider heroin, for example (bearing in mind that sex and love turn on the same parts of the brain as heroin). An occasional user will quickly find that one bag of snorted heroin isn't enough—that the brain now requires seven bags to create the same effect that one once had. Before long, snorting the heroin no longer offers the intense rush that we want and feel we *need*. So we shoot the heroin into our veins. Eventually a *ceiling effect* kicks in. Maybe seven bags of heroin offer the effect we crave but more than ten bags is too much. Suffice it to say that by the time we reach the porn equivalent of seven bags of heroin, porn is probably messing up our lives and our relationships.

It's interesting to consider whether society itself helps tolerance. For instance, in 2016 *Playboy*, the magazine that many young men used to stash in their closets, stopped publishing pictures of nude women. The reason? Lack of interest! It seems nudie magazines just couldn't compete with the live action so readily available online. And as we see, year after year what we can view on the internet defies the boundaries of the year before. What was once a huge turn-on for us now becomes boring. We develop tolerance. This means your addicted state of mind, watching intense and novel scenes, is the new normal.

Withdrawal

A key feature of some addictions is withdrawal. When you get addicted, the reward and reasoning centers of the brain become hijacked so that the addictive object no longer creates pleasure or a high; instead, the object becomes necessary to regain a sense of feeling normal. Take away the seven bags of heroin from the seven-bags-daily user, and they will experience excruciating withdrawal: body aches, horrible nausea with vomiting, diarrhea, shivers, leg cramps, involuntary movements of the legs (referenced by the term kicking the habit), and cold goose-flesh skin (responsible for the phrase going cold turkey). Addicts describe the sensations as the worst pain imaginable. Similarly (in concept although not severity), when you take away porn from a person who has developed a tolerance and has become habituated to using it, they experience a kind of withdrawal. That withdrawal manifests itself in the person's loss of sexual desire and sexual capabilities in nonpornographic situations.

What Qualifies as an Emotional Affair?

What happens when men and women, or people who are attracted to each other, are best friends, the relationships are deep and loving, and there is no sex involved? Everyone has their own opinion, but here are some signs of trouble:

- The friendship, or at least the extent of it, is kept secret from your spouse.
- The relationship is filled with stolen moments of longing and complaints about each other's romantic partners.
- The relationship competes with and undermines the primary relationship.

In these circumstances the relationship no longer qualifies as *just* a friendship, even if sex is not (overtly) on the table. At that point it qualifies as an *emotional affair.*

Emotional affairs are controversial. Some mental health experts claim that a lack of sexual contact means there's no affair or issue of betrayal. But those of us who work with patients whose infidelity troubles often lead to divorce have another perspective. Even if sex never happens, the intensity of an emotional bond with another can create a schism between primary partners that can feel even more invasive and threatening than a purely sexual affair.

Emotional affairs can be intense, taking the place of marital relationships when close connections develop that rival the marriage with feelings of deep emotional attachment and shared confidences and that offer acceptance, comfort, and support. So what is an emotional affair? In sum, an intense, intimate, and secret relationship that competes with and undermines the marriage. For every person and every marriage that means something different.

Am I Having an Emotional Affair?

How can you tell if you're having an emotional affair? The first telltale sign: you keep the nature and extent of your connection with the other person secret from your spouse. Your spouse may even know the person, yet gradually you talk to your partner less and less about the intensity of the connection. The emotional affair has deep intimacy, your conversations with the affair part-ner are peppered with complaints about your primary relation-ship, you look forward to communicating with the affair partner more than with your spouse, and your affair partner is someone who might be otherwise sexually and emotionally attractive to you. The lack of sex may help you feel a sense of propriety while developing a deeper and more meaningful connection.

So what's the difference between an emotional affair and a friendship? In an emotional affair, sex is not on the table but is generally under the table. One or both partners feel that "if only we had the opportunity," or "if only we were brave enough," or "if only we weren't married, we would be the per-fect couple." The sexual and romantic tensions are sometimes palpable or sometimes utterly unconscious. In my clinical practice, the key to my definition of an emotional affair is that it undermines your primary relationship. Close friends are people who you bring into your circle. Instead of taking the place of your spouse emotionally, friends join you and your spouse for holidays, vacations, and family dinners. Emotional affair partners hurt your marriage.

Our discussion and deconstruction of the nature of emo-tional affairs gets at the very heart of why people cheat. When we look at affairs in which people fall in love without sex—not unlike an old-fashioned romance, if you will—we are seeing the essence of what intense affairs are all about. This examination also highlights common differences between how men and women often view and engage in emotional affairs as well as the personality traits that amplify or diminish their perceptions of infidelity.

How Our Minds Talk Us into Emotional Affairs

Just as we saw in the arena of virtual affairs, the forces of the brain's powerful reward system's intense longings trigger and reinforce emotional affairs. From a neuroscience point of view, the emotional affair begins to take on an addictive quality, igniting the neural circuitry associated with love, desire, and validation. Neurologically speaking, the emotional connection that develops is no different from falling in love without sex—although often sex follows.

But that doesn't need to be the case, of course. Understanding the mechanisms of emotional infidelity offers a powerful defense against the groundswell of intoxicating forces that, if left unchecked, could lead to the unintended demise of your primary relationship. Identifying the addictive qualities of the heated mix of emotions that in the moment can feel so captivating can help keep you from getting caught up. Instead, thinking it through from a brain-science level can help you recognize the sometimes-toxic patterns at play before they completely take over, keeping an affair from either developing or progressing.

Similarly, making sense of the psychology that can facilitate infidelity can help us better understand both our partners and ourselves. In order to comprehend this we must first grasp the psychological process called *splitting*. This term describes our tendency—part of our human nature—to attribute mostly positive traits to one person while attributing mostly negative traits to another. We saw this with Laura, who called her husband a pig while lionizing the elevator man.

Only people with serious personality disorders get stuck in severe and unforgiving overall assessments of people as all good or all bad. Healthy people, meanwhile, can see the good and bad in most people. My point here is that splitting is a normal dynamic that operates in the everyday lives of healthy people and routinely occurs in love relationships. As we see throughout this book, splitting is a key psychological mechanism at play in emotional affairs.

Perhaps splitting is common to the human condition because we must figure out who to trust and who to distrust. Evolution has required us to draw close ties to family, friends, and our tribe. Protecting those close ties necessitates that we differentiate between *us* and *them*. Splitting is our brain's fast-track system for quickly deciding who is with us and who is against us. The irrationality and absurdity of splitting with a long-term partner is clear: How can we adore someone one year and shun them the next? Yet this unconscious process remains a part of our human nature.

Splitting a complex, multifaceted human being into an all-good or all-bad person involves what psychoanalysts call *idealization* and *devaluation*. In many cases when an affair, sexual or otherwise, is brewing, the person straying idealizes the affair partner. The object of your desire seems too good to be true because s/he *is*—because, in actuality, you have imbued another with all your hopes and dreams and set them out to be the answer to your deepest desires. Idealization is just part and parcel to falling in love.

Falling *out* of love, conversely, is characterized by *devaluation*: seeing the bad in your spouse so much that they become, in your mind, intolerable. They feel toxic. You feel the need to escape. Early on in your relationship your spouse was the one you idealized, the one who could do no wrong. Yet now, somehow, as you get further and further entwined in an emotional affair, your long-term partner can suddenly do no right. Here again we see the musical chairs of relationships.

How Do Men and Women Respond to Emotional vs. Sexual Affairs?

Before I delve into the data about how gender and personality traits affect individuals' perceptions of infidelity, a disclaimer: as I write this, seismic sexual and relationship shifts are unfolding in our society. For better or worse, romantic and sexual relationships are in greater flux than ever before. The roles and psychologies of men and women are changing in the home, in the workplace, and in romantic relationships of all kinds.

At one time women cheated half as often as men. Now millennial women in particular espouse a sense of sexual agency virtually unknown to women of an earlier time. Today young women openly and publicly engage in sexual experiences—from one-night stands to group sex—that decades earlier would have led to serious social consequences or ostracism for women.

Increasingly, same-gender couples have now ventured out of the closet and into the bride/bridegrooms' suite, and their experiences in marriage are likely to influence how our culture as a whole thinks not only about marriage but also about extramarital affairs. As male and female roles change, our sexuality and psychologies change too, along with the ways in which we conceptualize notions of fidelity and infidelity. With the caveat that existing data is based on what has happened in the past, here's what we think we know now.

Studies conducted among college students in the 1990s and early 2000s have shown that women, by and large, are more upset by their partner having an emotional affair, whereas men, most often, are more upset by a physical one. Researchers cite evolution as the reason for this difference. Evolutionary psychologists believe that, at their biological roots, these different reactions stem from paternity uncertainty among men and fear of resource reallocation among women. The argument states that men get more distressed by their partners' sexual infidelity than emotional infidelity because that sexual contact could lead them to devote resources to the offspring of another man. Women, however, who can be certain that their offspring is theirs, instead fear that if their mate becomes emotionally attached to another woman, he may withdraw his support, diverting resources to that woman's offspring instead. By this reasoning, sexual transgression carries more weight for men, whereas emotional transgression is more problematic for women. The research bears this out.

Three related studies seeking to test the evolutionary hypothesis confirmed that betrayed women were more upset by their husband developing emotional connections, whereas betrayed men focused on extramarital sex. In 1992 researchers documented these varying responses by examining physiological reactions, including measuring pulse, skin, and electric activity. Women showed a greater physiological response to emotional infidelity than men did to sexual infidelity.

It's hardly a news flash to say that, typically speaking, men are more focused on sex and women on emotion and attachment. As some researchers have explained, "men derive relatively more self-esteem from their sex lives, whereas women's self-esteem is more contingent on romantic commitment." Studies also suggest, however, that it's not just about gender but also about what each individual values. For example, one study showed that men who generally prioritized sex in romantic relationships as especially important experienced more distress when confronted with the discovery of a sexual affair, whereas men who placed less value on sex overall felt less distress.

How Often Does an Emotional Affair Become Sexual?

While there is no reliable body of scientific evidence about how often emotional affairs become physical, my clinical experience suggests it occurs quite often. A survey conducted by Dr. Shirley Glass found that 80 percent of emotional affairs between men and women progress into physical ones. Regardless of the exact figure, common sense dictates that among the worst ways to heal a relationship in crisis is by complicating it with a third person. Still, when that does happen, reason must prevail.

In the final analysis, all affairs—regardless of whether they're overtly sexual—are *emotional.* That's because all affairs are made in the mind. Why and how people cheat is as complicated as any aspect of human experience. Acts of infidelity are driven by people's hopes and dreams as well as by the anxieties and fears that they're trying to overcome through cultivating an outside relationship. Even as they may be more concerned than men about emotional affairs, women seem (based on the literature and collective clinical experience, because no hard data or reliable statistics currently exist) far more likely to get entangled in nonsexual, emotional affairs.

Emotional Affairs Can Be a Sign of Troubled Waters

Emotional affairs are often a sign of turbulence in the primary relationship. One study of 345 college students, plus 115 people in the surrounding community, found that affairs with a high degree of emotional involvement most often occur when people are discontented with their partners. Emotionally intimate affairs happened most often when, prior to the affair, the person cheating was already dissatisfied with the intimacy in his or her primary relationship. People who strayed reported that their needs for intimacy and for improved self-esteem fueled their infidelity. And those who felt unhappy in their current relationships also tended to feel less guilt about cheating. The research reinforces what I've seen clinically: emotionally involved affairs—regardless of whether they become sexual—actually present a greater danger for primary relationships than casual ones, more often leading to the primary relationship ending.

The take-home message here is that if you or your partner has forged an intense, secret connection with someone outside your relationship, consider that a big flashing warning sign that your partnership probably needs attention. You might think that if you only share an emotional and not a physical connection with another person, it won't matter for your relationship. But, in fact, the emotional intimacy with someone who's not your spouse might actually matter even more than a physical one! If you or your partner has already crossed the line into emotional affair territory, take heart: how to fix yourself and mend your relationship is precisely what we'll discuss in Part III.

chapter 6

The sex quest for
threesomes and orgies

As we learned in the chapter on desire, drop a new rat in a cage with rats who have just finished copulating, and the spent rats, males and females alike, will all suddenly tap a new reserve of energy for a new partner. The same seems to be true of people. It's one of the basic reasons people cheat. We like novelty. Sometimes people don't just want another partner as much as they want another experience, something that seems to be off the menu at home. In the next two chapters we'll talk about some specific examples of how this quest for novelty takes shape as well as the psychology and neuroscience that underlie it.

You're dating a man for six months, or maybe you're married for ten years, and then he says, "There something I always wanted to do." You love him dearly, and there's almost nothing you wouldn't do to make him happy. Then he announces that he wants to invite your best friend into the bedroom. How do you respond? The fact that his request is among the top male fantasies may or may not reassure you.

Maybe you're open to the idea. Or maybe you're the one who suggested it in the first place. Why not head to one of the many sex clubs in America's major cities where you can find an orgy? Or make your way online to start searching for a third?

With everyday life dominated by shared, mundane responsibilities, the idea of an additional playmate can be a special turn-on—an exciting diversion. Generally speaking, the familiar makes us feel secure, while the forbidden turns us on. For some a threesome might seem like the perfect solution. We get to have sex with our love while also enjoying more body parts as we sample otherwise forbidden fruit. Such adventures might not feel like cheating, as they include your partner, but from what I've seen in my practice, acting out this fantasy—or even trying to—can sometimes lead to as much heartbreak as infidelity.

Threesomes, as Old as Sex

The first known sex manual, the *Kama Sutra*, written in 400 BC, offers advice on threesomes and double penetration. A thousand years later, orgies were depicted in stone carvings on the walls of eleventh-century temples in India as instructive tools. The Renaissance brought renewed popular interest in threesomes, and at the center of the movement, in eighteenth-century Venice, Giacomo Casanova (aka Casanova), an erudite man of the arts known to Voltaire, Goethe, Mozart, and Pope Clement XIII, wrote extensively about his romances, starting with losing his virginity to two teenaged sisters. By the early 1970s many porn films featured group sex as the grand finale, and swinger parties became the scandal of suburban life. By the twenty-first century the trend seemed to have fallen off—at least according to claims by Pornhub that during the sixty-four million daily visits worldwide to their porn videos, "group sex" had sunk to number fourteen, between "ebony" and "lesbian scissoring."

Despite the popularity of swinging in the 1980s, twenti-eth-century psychiatrists did not endorse this novelty. Murray Bowen, one of the founders of the practice of couples' therapy, argued that triangulating a relationship with a threesome was rarely helpful to the couple. Another psychiatrist wrote in 1978 that sharing your partner with a third is an act of "pathological tolerance," meaning an unhealthy acceptance of a partner's re-quest. According to psychoanalytic post-Freudian theory, the threesome reenacts past trauma and jealousies, meaning that the essence of what makes it thrilling is the way it combines our fears and our desires. The threesome can become a little opera that we create to play with various emotions: our wish for a new playmate, our fear of losing our partner to another, our quest for the power to order our partner to succumb to another, and even our perverse quest for our own humiliation at seeing our lover with someone else. That combination of fear and desire—our pursuit of both power and psychic pain—can be not only enticing and erotic but also dangerous and destructive.

By the twenty-first century, however, medical opinion had changed to include greater acceptance of all sorts of what had been called *alternative lifestyles*. Studies of gay men, for example, found relatively little harm and even potential benefit to their primary relationships when partners engaged in consensual threesomes. When nonmonogamous heterosexual people engaging in group sex were assessed through psychological tests, they were found to be as mentally healthy as monogamous people. In fact, couples in open relationships having consensual sex outside of marriage were more likely to engage in safe-sex practices like using a condom when compared to unfaithful couples who said they were monogamous but cheated.

So How Common Is Group Sex, Anyway?

In the media there are many stories of healthy swinging, swapping, and threesomes. Partnered people have reported that group sex improved their marriage and stopped them from cheating behind their partners' backs. Shows like *Mad Men*, *Girls*, *American Horror Story*, *Young Pope*, *Game of Thrones*, and *House of Cards* have all featured threesome moments. Sarah Ruhl's 2017 play *How to Transcend a Happy Marriage*, is a tale of sexual awakening through the eyes of one middle-aged woman who swaps with her friends.

Although there is little data on middle-aged people, some reasonable studies on college students shed light on threesome experiences. Researchers who surveyed 274 Canadian heterosexual undergraduates reported that 81 percent of men and 32 percent of women said they were interested in threesomes, and 20 percent and 8 percent, respectively, said they had participated in a threesome. The men were twice as likely to have had an experience with two women, whereas the heterosexual women surveyed were equally divided between those who had been involved with two men and those with two women.

The researchers concluded, "A threesome with two women is the ultimate fantasy of many heterosexual men, a conquest above all conquests, a fun, playful party time, and twice the number of all the body parts they enjoy sexually. The same kind of threesome doesn't necessarily have the same specific appeal to a heterosexual woman, beyond a general excitement that a group sex scenario would afford."

In 2016 in the United States researchers surveyed 196 undergraduates at a large southeastern university. They found that 15 percent of the sample had experienced a threesome, with men suggesting the idea nearly twice as often as women. In most of the encounters the third was a female friend of the woman in the couple. The men overwhelmingly felt it was a more positive experience than the women did. It appeared that 10 percent of the time the men had repeatedly pressured their female partners into the threesome. Research found that, by and large, men had defined the sexual situation ("this is going to be an exciting sexual adventure"), named the actors ("you and I can find someone to make a threesome hot"), and plotted behaviors ("let's ask your former roommate to come over—we can get liquored up and see if she is up for a threesome"). Similar to the Canadian researchers, the American study authors wrote, "Men are socialized early to be sexual, to be sexually aggressive, and to be involved in sexual variety. The data for this study reflect higher interest by men, aggressiveness, and participation in having a threesome than reported by women."

An estimated one-third of men have a threesome on their bucket list, whereas only a small percentage of women say the same. One can imagine, however, that as cultural shifts lead women to become more sexually empowered, young women may themselves grow up to be more aggressive about pursuing group sex with both same-sex and mixed-sex configurations.

Group Sex and the Novelty-Seeking Brain

The main reason I want to talk about threesomes in this book is to further our discussion of the psychology and neuroscience of our search for novel sexual experiences. When it comes to thrill seeking, we're not all the same. Some of us shy away from novelty: we like the same thing for breakfast, and we want to go on the same vacations and sleep with the same lovers. Others, particularly philanderers, get bored easily: they don't want just one cup of coffee to wake up in the morning; they want as many caffeine jolts as they can pack in before bedtime. And sexually, they want new turn-ons.

Much of cheating has to do with our quest to fulfill a fantasy outside of what we traditionally do with our partner in bed. For some this impulse to pursue novelty seems to be coded into their genes. As we'll discuss in detail, scientists have identified genes associated with risky and sensation-seeking behaviors, including gambling and drug abuse as well as risky investments and dangerous pastimes like parachuting and, of course, having many sexual partners. Multiple studies over the past twenty years have supported this finding, but we have still only scratched the surface.

The Dopamine Well

Ten years ago Dr. Mary Jeanne Kreek, an addiction teacher of mine at Cornell and Rockefeller Universities, wrote in the journal *Nature Neuroscience*, "Genetic variation may partially underlie complex personality and physiological traits—such as impulsivity, risk taking and stress responsivity—as well as a substantial proportion of vulnerability to addictive diseases." Specifically here she was explaining why some of us are prone to taking the risk of using hard drugs that lead to addictions, but the same research applies to risk-taking in sex.

In 1996 Dr. Dean Hamer, in his article "Population and Familial Association Between the D4 Dopamine Receptor Gene and Measures of Novelty Seeking," published what was possibly the first molecular association to a personality trait reported in the literature. He found that what we call thrill seeking, sensation seeking, or risk taking is associated with alterations in what's called the *dopamine receptor gene*—the gene that orchestrates how the brain receives and processes the reward chemical dopamine. A researcher at the National Institutes for Health, Hamer discovered that people with altered dopamine genes tend to seek unusual sex.

When I spoke with him, Dr. Hamer explained that dopamine specifically seems to affect how likely you are to wind up "having sex for kicks." Although dopamine receptors don't seem to influence your love for your partner, they do influence how eager you are for an extramarital or new sexual experience. "What was interesting is that the strongest link was to 'unusual' partners considering the subject's sexual orientation, a clear sign that the gene was acting through its influence on the desire for novelty." He found this dopamine alteration specifically among people who have sexual encounters out of their norm, such as gay people who have straight sex and straight people who have gay sex. Straight men who have this dopamine gene that is associated with high-novelty seekers were "six times more likely to have slept with another man than those with a short gene." Conversely, self-described gay men had sex with more than five times as many women as did those with the short, low novelty-seeking form.

Dr. Justin Garcia and his colleagues at Binghamton University confirmed this association between dopamine genes and infidelity. In 2010 they studied 197 young adults and found that men and women with longer dopamine genes had more one-night stands. With findings similar to Dr. Hamer's, Dr. Garcia reported that people with the long dopamine gene "don't have more sex, but they are more likely to have infidelity and casual sex." The long-gene folks, he added, weren't just one-time adulterers either; instead, they tended to cheat more often.

It is not, clarified Dr. Garcia, that more promiscuous thrill seekers have more dopamine in their bodies; instead, their particular type of dopamine receptors require more dopamine to have the same effect as that experienced by a non-thrill-seeking person. For them to get a rush, they require more sensation-seeking behaviors to kick up their dopamine levels. Think of this dopamine receptor like a big well that can contain lots of water: the well doesn't function properly until it is filled all the way up. And what fills up these long dopamine receptors is lots of excitement.

How we negotiate our differing desires for novelty is what keeps marriage therapists in business. Most couples find middle ground, and both people compromise. Some relationships, often those based on power or financial leverage, have one partner reigning supreme, with the more powerful partner taking the attitude, *Why should we* both *be unhappy?* Some relationships require one partner to tiptoe around and avoid certain areas of conflict in order to not offend their more sensitive partner. How you compromise and what you compromise on is up to you. But compromise and forgiveness strike me as the best recipe for lasting love.

Joe's story: A thrill-seeking brain

Joe is a perfect example of a thrill seeker. Fast cars, fast women, group sex with male and female partners alike—all these things had turned him on for as long as he could recall. He loved his wife. Early in their marriage her willingness to have sex in public places turned him on. Joe loved taking risks and novel stimulation. He took out large loans with personal guarantees that would cause most of us to lose sleep. Chancy investments with a big potential upside fired him up. So did driving a sports car at 140 mph. What would scare most people sent a charge to Joe's brain. Without taking chances, without doing something new, Joe felt dead inside.

His hunger for novelty led to an affair with a subordinate in his office. After three years, as he packed his bags to leave his wife for his new playmate, he suddenly realized that his wife was his true love. The two recommitted to their relationship, but before long he con-vinced her that, to spice things up, they should go to swinger parties and find people online for group sex.

Joe liked the thrill of new things—someone else's penis dangling in front of his face, his wife performing oral sex on another man. He loved to explore new women. He just had this extreme yearning for novel experiences.

Although most of us relish surprise and even a bit of danger, Joe's need for new stimuli led him to engage in compulsive sexuality, which stemmed, at least in part, from his attention deficit disorder, or ADD. It's important to keep in mind that risk taking is not a psychiatric ill-ness. However, a few psychiatric illnesses *are* associated with risky behavior, including ADD. It is well established in the medical literature that sexually compulsive people often have ADD problems. It's no accident that many of my patients who are compulsive philanderers also have ADD.

Although going into the details of ADD and other psychiatric disorders is beyond the scope of this book, a brief discussion might help shed some light on the neuroscientific mechanisms involved with novelty seeking. ADD is commonly perceived as a difficulty with focusing on schoolwork, but it's actually a hallmark of a brain that desperately needs intense stimulation. This is why people like Joe—and many of my other patients—end up getting bored with vanilla sex. Without sufficient stimulation for their brains, they blank out. They need much more of a turn-on to get turned on. As much of the research demonstrates, there's a subset of people, both men and women, whose threshold for thrill is beyond the normal appetite.

Our treatment plan for Joe included carefully reviewing the pros and cons of his desires, an approach called *cognitive behavioral psychotherapy.* He progressed despite a few slips in which he went as far as contemplating and arranging a group-sex rendezvous, though he did not follow through. A big moment in his recovery came on the eve of his forty-fifth birthday. He came to see me one day with tears in his eyes. His wife had just organized a surprise party for him. "I don't know why she puts up with me," he said, shaking his head.

"She loves you," I responded.

"Look at all the bad I've done," Joe continued. "It's crazy. It's really crazy how I've cheated and fucked around. Throughout the party I thought, what a heel. It's never been clearer to me, in this moment. I can't say I won't want to do what I did again or ever think about. But what a lucky son-of-a-bitch am I!" Joe was learning what it meant to be faithful.

Although Joe had been able to talk his wife into a few swingers meetings before he reshaped his priorities, another patient of mine, Sam, was not so lucky; instead, his relentless pursuit of a threesome ended an intense, loving relationship, and he wound up alone.

Sam and Erika's story: A cautionary tale

After splitting with their spouses, fortysomethings Sam and Erika met on a dating site and quickly fell in love. They courted each other over dinners in Italian restaurants and romanced in dark jazz clubs. A month into their relationship they planned a rendezvous in a luxurious hotel room so they could make love overlooking a New York City park. They spent the summer months playing tennis and lying naked on the grass at Sam's beach house, staring at the stars. They shared their love of the arts. They both felt they'd found their soul mate and couldn't imagine being with anyone else for the rest of their lives.

Their relationship was going great until Sam decided it was time to spice things up and started hinting about his secret desire for a threesome. He frequently tried to insert suggestions about having another woman or man in the bedroom. While they were making love, in the heat of the moment, Sam would ask Erika if she would want a third. And in the heat of the moment she said she would try it.

At one point, because she loved Sam and wanted him to be happy, Erika entertained the idea of asking a friend of hers to join them, but she got cold feet. "No problem," Sam told her. Soon thereafter Sam found a sex workshop for them to attend that featured instruction on sexual techniques and encouraged the swapping of partners during the sexual homework assignments to be done in the evening. Erika sensed Sam's desire to have sex with strangers, and the idea upset her so much that it made her cry. In the end they completed their homework assignments alone, and as always, their lovemaking was spectacular and passionate.

But Sam was relentless. He told Erika he had heard about another sex seminar focused on clitoral massage. Sam said he only wanted to do it with Erika. They entered a classroom of about three dozen strangers. After a couple of hours of massage instruction the women in the room were instructed to disrobe from the waist down and sit by the side of a man, many of whom they'd just met. With rubber gloves and lube, the man was to massage the woman's clitoris under the guidance of roving instructors who wandered between the couples and supervised their stroking, much like a high school woodshop teacher might inspect and guide students' carpentry efforts. Erika and Sam stayed together during the clitoral massage, but Erika could tell that Sam wanted to do it with a stranger or have a stranger massage her.

Although Sam tried to downplay his desires, he persisted in feeling that he needed to experience what he had always watched in porn. Especially as she could read him so well, Erika sensed his yearning. Whenever he had the chance, Sam hinted about having her friends join them in the bedroom. From Sam's point of view, Erika was his soul mate, and sex with her was the best he'd ever had. Erika felt the same way. Still, he wanted more. He sought sexual nirvana before he died. Sexual fulfillment. The kind of ideal that magazines discuss and that the new sexual mores suggest is available to everyone. People, you can have it all!

As he pushed for some notion of sexual perfection, Erika got fed up. When she left him, Sam was mystified. "We love each other so," Sam told me. "Couldn't she just do a little more for me?" Meanwhile Erika had given more than she could comfortably give. She wound up feeling insecure, unloved, and unappreciated and that she could never be enough for Sam.

In treatment my job was to help Sam realize that if you push hard enough, sooner or later you end up pushing your partner off a cliff, a plummet from which they can never recover. Once Erika had felt his fantasy as a personal rejection, she couldn't bounce back. Sam didn't recognize the problem until it was too late. Hounding his love in pursuit of his fantasy destroyed the best relationship either of them had known.

For the common scenario of lusting after another and inviting a team of lovers into your bedroom, there is no easy answer, no simple solution. Most couples define romance and love as wanting nothing but each other. But that ideal is actually at odds with the reality of most long-term relationships. In other words, many of us solve the problem of lusting for another by pretending, lying, cheating, or just ignoring. I'd argue that better solutions are possible. At the very least I recommend an honest, well-intended, and respectful exchange of ideas as well as explicit compromise and sacrifice for the sake of your relationship. Compromise, compromise, and compromise some more, making real sacrifices for each other's happiness, might be what real love is all about.

We'll dig into this approach more deeply in Part III, but for now let's continue our exploration of the human sex quest for novelty. Next up: bondage and other kink.

chapter 7

When pain is pleasure,
and other kink

One reason people cheat is that they're hungry for something they can't get at home. Many of my patients who have had extramarital flings ventured out because they wanted a taste of *kink*, today's term for unconventional sexual behaviors between consenting adults. Also known as *BDSM* (bondage, domination, sadism, and masochism), which involves role-playing domination and submission, kink can include a variety of interests and activities, such as *voyeurism* (getting sexually excited by watching others), *exhibitionism* (getting turned on by having others see you in a sexual position), and *fetishism* (gratification linked to a single, nongenital body part or object for sexual excitement, such as the foot or an item of clothing).

Kink often involves flirting with the forbidden. But gauging exactly which proclivities fall into the category of "unconventional" isn't easy, especially because more than 50 percent of all psychologically normal men and women enjoy some form of sexual activity that hints of domination or submission. This 50 percent figure challenges the very definition of kink, however, revealing that what society considers "conventional" depends on cultural norms that shift over time. One example of how conventions change is the role of the vibrator, an object used for sexual stimulation once thought to be fetishistic but now considered a part of normal sex. (Today more than half of US women report having used a vibrator.)

Society's Prejudices

We can't separate a conversation about kink from a discussion of American society's prejudices. In the past, mental health professionals took a very negative stance toward anything kinky. For the better part of the past few centuries educated society, with the imprimatur of doctors and the clergy, set firm guidelines for what was considered healthy sex. One of the most influential early sexologists of the last century, Dr. Richard von Krafft-Ebing, taught that anything but foreplay leading to vaginal intercourse between a man and woman was sick. No exaggeration!

In 1906 he wrote, "with opportunity for the natural satisfaction of the sexual instinct, every expression of it that does not correspond with the purpose of nature—i.e., procreation—must be regarded as perverse." His classic *Psychopathia*

Sexualis: eine Klinisch-Forensische Studie (*Sexual Psychopathy: A Clinical-Forensic Study*) popularized the term *sadism* based on the sexual cruelty of the aristocratic writer Marquis de Sade (1740–1814) and *masochism* based on the romantic misogynist writer Leopold Ritter von Sacher-Masoch, author of *Venus in Furs* (1869).

BDSM wasn't the only now-normalized sexual practice that organized medicine once called a disease. The list of ill-begotten diagnoses and treatments is legendary. Nineteenth-century doctors were so confused about female sexuality that some doctors *themselves* manually stimulated women to treat their "hysteria" (now known as anxiety). Vibrators were said to have been invented in 1880 by Dr. Joseph Mortimer Granville, a physician known to treat female hysteria, in order to rest his busy hands from giving women genital massages. While hysteria or anxiety was thought to require medical intervention in the form of a vibrator-induced orgasm, women who robustly sought their own clitoral orgasms were considered sick. Women whose sexual appetites rivaled men were said to suffer from the disease *nymphomania*. As I mentioned in the chapter on desire, homosexuality was considered a mental illness as recently as thirty years ago. Essentially, organized medicine sanctioned many of society's sexual prejudices.

Thankfully, we are better informed today, and our culture is more enlightened. In the twentieth century, researchers administered psychological tests to people who were into BDSM and found that these novel-sex seekers were as normal (and abnormal) as everyone else. Today, for most couples, dabbling in kink is commonplace. This kind of play often includes a bite, a slap on the rear, or using a loose-fitting belt or silk scarf to simulate helplessness and domination through being tied up. Although some kinky play doesn't call for much planning, experience, or equipment, other practices are more intense, requiring a certain level of expertise coupled with acting ability that, even if not always available at home, can easily be found online.

Before we delve further into kink, we need to distinguish it from unlawfully trying to dominate another person. Unlike kink, which is by nature consensual, sexual activities thrust upon unsuspecting people (like a flasher who exposes himself in the park) are not kink but rather sexual offenses punishable by law. In this chapter I'm only discussing sex among consenting and competent adults. Although the practitioners of kink discussed here may keep their activities secret from their spouses, they do not commit sex offenses.

When Kink Comes Up in Relationships

Shaking things up in the bedroom by talking about or trying out kinky activities can, of course, bring some couples together in new, unexpected ways. Other times, though, instead of opening a door to a spicy path of newfound adventure for couples, kink drives a wedge into relationships.

For an unsuspecting spouse, first learning about a partner's desires for kinky activities years into a relationship can be quite a shocker. The desire for kink can lead to lying, motivate infidelity, and wind up prompting feelings of guilt and betrayal. The situation can end up even further complicated when a spouse offers to try the kinky sex acts their partner desires only to be rejected. Sometimes kink is only a turn-on if it is performed with strangers or professionals or in forbidden venues, thus excluding the spouse from being the person who can fulfill their partner's desires in the bedroom.

For nonkink lovers, it can be extremely difficult to understand the draw of certain fetishes like, say, foot worship or lashings with a whip, especially when you learn that it's some-thing your spouse of twenty years has been actively craving. But the first step toward mending fences is understanding.

Despite the object of one's desire, regardless of the par-ticular version of someone's preferred kink, it's important to recognize the neurochemical pull that these desires have on a person. There's no simple answer to what draws someone toward kink. Certainly novelty seeking and a predisposition toward risk taking play a role, as we discussed earlier; most people who are into BDSM say they enjoy the intensity of playing forbidden games with specific rules of conduct. Al-though participants role play around submission and sadism, both partners are actually in control of the situation through the use of agreed-upon "safe words" that signal when to ease up or stop. They toy with the lack of control, but in essence, all participants are always and ultimately steering the experience and can stop it at any time.

Most BDSM participants are either *tops* (dominant) or *bot-toms* (submissive), although a few switch between the two roles. In studies both tops and bottoms report that their play is not only enjoyable but also leaves them feeling better, less stressed, and closer to their play partner after the BDSM experience.

However, for a very small percentage of my patients with strong BDSM desires, a few may have been beaten physically or mentally brow beaten by a parent or by peers growing up. From a psychological perspective, their desire to submit may stem from a need to work through earlier traumas. In my experience these people are not looking for their long-term partners to join them in BDSM play; instead, many seek for-bidden rendezvous to reenact humiliating experiences that, by definition, can't be satisfying if done in the context of a loving and committed partnership. They are looking for a stranger to create the aura of supreme and real domination or submission that can't exist in most long-term relationships. Those people often turn to adulterous liaisons to fulfill their cravings.

Accepting the Reality of Your Mind

Sexual desires—regardless of whether we are proud of them, like them, or even accept them—are a part of us. They develop early in our lives, between the ages of five and twenty, and they're often with us for a lifetime. Recall the *path in the forest* metaphor I used to describe how our minds chart the course for our sexual desires, like forging a new trail in an overgrown woods. Each time we repeat the same thought or action, the path becomes that much more firmly set.

Many of our sexual desires surface before our tenth birthday and then grow in intensity during our teenage years. These desires get cemented in our psyches, appearing each time we're aroused. They show up when we get turned on, when we masturbate, and when we engage in sex with a partner. **Like a forest, with weeds and overgrowth that get trampled down over time, the pathways of the mind take root, and it's not easy to carve out a new trail that's different from the one you've been trekking on for a lifetime.** Eventually, new paths of desire and arousal can be established in the brain, but it takes time. Many of my patients want to change overnight. Part of my job is to help them develop patience with themselves and recognize the difficulty of reshaping desires.

Whether you ultimately decide that your fantasies and desires are right or wrong, healthy or unhealthy, welcome or repulsive, it's important to understand that you can't easily change them. Instead, learning to manage our impulses

David's story: Submissive desires

My patient David desired submission in the form of foot worship and humiliation. Even in the safety of his psychiatrist's office he was shy about confessing that what turned him on was being bound and then forced to lie on the floor to lick and smell a woman's feet. He also took pleasure in getting whipped and penetrated anally with a dildo. Like so many high-powered men and women, what David sought through BDSM encounters was the chance *not* to have to be the strong, take-charge person he was in the rest of his life. What enticed him was escape from his everyday existence.

David had been a firm, take-charge father to his five now-grown children, and he had been a (mostly) good husband to his wife of twenty-two years, with whom he'd enjoyed a life of shared values and interests, mutual respect, and a great sex life overall. But none of that gave David what he craved: the chance to wash, fondle, and smell women's feet. He first recognized his foot fetish in early adulthood and had always found female feet more erotic than their genitals. When he began dating, David sometimes came across women who would occasionally indulge his desire to caress their feet. His wife, a loving partner, indulged him as well, willingly participating in foot worship sometimes before intercourse.

But at a certain point David craved more than his wife could provide, and he began turning to paid sex workers whom he contacted online. His wife was no match for the professionals paid to play this game daily. The comfort of the family home and bedroom did not offer the thrill of danger in the neighborhoods he would travel to, the grittiness of the encounter, and the uncertainties that raised his pulse and felt like a roller-coaster ride about to begin.

Long before he arrived at the rendezvous he felt great excitement in planning the encounter. He would read through dozens of profiles.

continues

He could feel his mind getting revved up as he drove to the dominatrix's (dom's) apartment. He could feel himself get more and more excited as he approached the venue.

As we've seen in our discussions of the brain's reward systems, the biology of anticipation is often the key to whether people act on their desires to cheat. The brain's response to anticipatory excitement about sex is a key catalyst to an affair. Very often what leads a person to cheat is not the actual sex but an eagerness for sex that can leave you feeling a desperate craving as your brain tricks you into believing that the forbidden fruit is your lifeline to nirvana.

By the time David descended the steps to a dom's lair, he had entered the *flow* state we discussed earlier—his mind focused, his heart pounding. As the door opened, his whole body tingled with nervous anticipation at the prospect of entering a world unlike anything in his normal life. Only later, when he stepped back out onto the street after his visits, did he worry about the dangerous and unpredictable situation into which he'd just put himself and grasp the threat to his safety and reputation.

The reasons for David's intense submissive desires never became completely clear. Was it just that he wanted more opportunities to take a backseat in life? Did he need to feel less in charge and strong all the time but not know how to acquire that in healthy ways? Did this tendency arise out of something that had happened in childhood?

David's desires might have stemmed from how his father treated him. When David was a child, his father took down David's pants and beat him publicly on the butt in front of the neighbors. Or maybe from when David was a youngster and two boys forcibly pulled down his pants in the woods. Could any of this have contributed to David's dysfunctional interest in BDSM? Maybe. There are myriad factors that determine our behavior, and it is nearly impossible to know how much our genes, our early exposures, our parents, and our experiences contribute to our sexuality. All that mattered to me was that David wanted to change.

As part of David's treatment, we talked through various possible psychological root causes. But we mainly focused on changing David's behavior. Without me judging him or his lusts, we agreed that he would try to modify his behaviors in order to get his life back on track. We discussed how giving up his escapades, with all their dangers, was a loss. I never told David what to do; I only encouraged him to consider modifying his behaviors based on what *he* had decided was the right new path for him.

David was able to focus on the benefits of modifying his behaviors. What made the changes stick was that he felt whole. He felt honest. He focused on his health and well-being. The time, effort, and money he had poured into his sexual outlets he now put toward working out and having more fun. He figured out other ways to deal with stress. David ended up gaining more than he'd given up.

A crucial element of David's treatment was exploring ways to create a more open and loving connection with his wife. Early in treatment I generally speak with a patient's spouse or significant other to find out what they believe the problem is and to enlist their support and help in the treatment—especially when the patient's issues are sexual, they often involve the significant other, and can't be addressed in isolation. When I met David's wife, a confident, intelligent woman who had David's best interest at heart, I advised her that the first step toward bridging the gap between them was for her to listen to her husband without judging or shaming him as he shared his desires.

David came clean with his wife, confessing his dalliances with doms. "I love my wife," he later reported. "It was a big gamble; the hardest thing I ever have done." Once David's wife saw that he was committed to her and their family, she supported him and incorporated his interest in kink into their own lovemaking. Inspired by his kinky imagination, she shared a few fantasies of her own. "My wife is very open-minded," he said, pausing and smiling. "I'm lucky."

continues

Like nearly all my patients, David was trying to do the right thing. He was determined to stop doing anything unfaithful or against his family's moral code, which meant no more BDSM prostitution. His wife committed to reinvigorating the marriage and engaging in more of the kinds of sex he wanted. Of course, his wife could not reproduce the danger or uncertainty of his past encounters, but she could participate with enthusiasm out of an earnest desire to please him. Soon her love took the place of the dangerous liaisons. David's relationship with his wife had reached the "best point ever." Now he enjoyed foot worship with her, plus a whole lot more. Was David living happily ever after with no desire for forbidden fruit? Of course not. He still looked at other women and still thought about cheating. Yet he made peace with his choices and lived according to his ideals.

toward troubling proclivities is key. In the short term I urge people to focus on their behavior. Over time, with effort, many people manage to chart a new course for their lusts.

Women Dig Kink Too

Experts used to think that kink was something only men wanted. Doctors said that the only women who would do anything intentionally and overtly kinky were prostitutes who were just in it for the money. That was the thinking of the nineteenth and twentieth century. But now we know differently.

Seeking to dispel the long-held myth that kink was a male-only activity of little interest to women, sociologist Jennifer Eva Rehor collected and analyzed data on 1,580 women regarding more than a hundred BDSM sexual activities. After recruiting most of her subjects from women-only kink events and through the internet, she found that of those she sampled, roughly twice as many women preferred nondangerous bottom, or masochistic, encounters to sadistic roles, although more than half said they sometimes switched roles between tops and bottoms. Although bondage was one of the most preferred activities, over 80 percent of the women surveyed preferred bondage in which they could readily get out if they wanted, as opposed to being unable to escape. More than 50 percent enjoyed being watched naked or having sex and 75 percent enjoyed what might be described as a fetishistic interest, such as finding a certain piece of lingerie, shoes, corset, or some sexy outfit arousing. Over 70 percent of the women surveyed enjoyed role-play scenarios such as master/slave and physical experiences like mild spanking and biting.

When I reached out to Dr. Patsy Evans, a therapist who specializes in kink, to learn more about women's experiences, she was quick to explain that most members of the kink community discourage infidelity and encourage participants to only engage in "ethical BDSM." This means no lying to or cheating on a partner. Part of her work involves counseling people on how to maintain these ethical BDSM standards. What gets my patients into trouble, however, is unethical kink, in which the long-term partner is kept in the dark.

Many people venture outside their marriage for kink, thinking that just as with an emotional affair, if no one is taking off their clothes, there is no harm in it. They convince themselves that there's no need to tell their long-term partner about this furtive rendezvous. However, just like with an emotional affair, what pulls couples apart is the secretive nature of this intense experience. The secret search for an extramarital thrill can be the forerunner of the end of the marriage. Even if the cheating

Evelyn's story: Build me a box

Evelyn, a forty-year-old woman with a longtime interest in very dominant men discovered in her late thirties how the world of BDSM could
help her take her desire to be dominated to new heights. Evelyn had
grown up in a loving family in the Midwest, done well in school, and
now had a successful career as an executive secretary. When she
and her husband first met, Evelyn was captivated by the way he—
at six-foot-two and all muscle—commanded the space whenever he
walked into a room. She loved his forceful penetrations during vaginal
sex. But after the birth of their child, their sex life fizzled. That's when
Evelyn sought gratification outside the marriage, starting an affair with
someone she met in a bar.

As happened in the movie *Fifty Shades of Grey*, Evelyn's affair
partner introduced her to BDSM. She found herself enjoying being
tied up, lightly beaten, and then having intercourse. She also took a
liking to sexually applied needles (small *butterfly* venipuncture needles inserted into her breasts and near her genitals) and light whip-
pings. As a teenager, Evelyn had been diagnosed with a disease of
the connective tissue that causes great pain. For her, part of the draw
of BDSM was that the pain that her partner lovingly administered
offset and reset the pain of her disease. "Better the pain you can
control," she said.

She explained it to me this way: "By no means get confused. The
bottom [submissive] is the one who controls the pain because they
are the one who can say stop or can say more, stronger." Some days
she hurt so much from her disease that she couldn't play. But on

other days, she said, "I want to hurt more because it cancels it out. It's almost like a high."

For Evelyn the sting from her dom's bullwhip or the mild electric shocks he delivered offered sensual delight that's more than an orgasm: "It's almost like being in a tunnel and you're floating and the only thing that's connected to you is another person."

After her affair with her first dom fizzled, Evelyn looked for a new thrill on the internet where sites like Alt.com (for BDSM and alternative lifestyles), Fetlife.com (for fetish life), and Kinkyjungle.com or participation in Facebook sex groups offer venues for finding kink playmates. Online is where Evelyn met her "Greek god," a forty-four-year-old ex-military officer. He was teaching her over Skype how to bind her feet to a chair when Evelyn wound up masturbating in front of him. Then they took their play further with encounters shared via web cam, using a vibrator, clothespins, and hot wax poured on her breasts. She says that her dom recognized that "I don't need to think out of the box. I need someone to *build me a box and put me in it*—someone to take charge again." Her dom literally put her on a schedule that included what and when she could eat. And Evelyn loved it.

Ultimately they started traveling to see each other, and their play crossed the flesh line to include in-person sex. Evelyn's marriage could not withstand her newfound relationship. Her husband could not provide the fresh excitement and control she wanted. She divorced him, and soon Evelyn and her Greek god made plans to live together in a committed relationship. Only time would tell if her new relationship would remain as gratifying once they were together on a daily basis.

partner thinks their "experience" will never lead them to leaving their spouse, the affair is often the first step toward separation. Taking steps toward healing as well as finding effective ways to manage our shifting desires are what we will discuss next in Part III.

part three

discovery, disclosure, and moving forward toward healing

There are few traumas in life as devastating as discovering that your partner has been cheating. I've had several patients contemplate suicide for the first time in their lives after learning of a spouse's infidelity. One ended up in a psychiatric hospital, tied to a gurney. Betrayal by a partner strikes deeply at our core and shakes our sense of the reality of our lives. In my experience such transgressions are among the worst, most traumatizing events that can happen to a person.

Especially given the trauma to the betrayed spouse, it is easy to take sides. To think of one person as a villain, the other, an innocent victim. We can treat discovering infidelity like uncovering a crime in which the criminal needs to be interrogated and punished while the victim deserves reparations. No doubt the person who does the cheating has wronged and betrayed the other, and the couple needs to address what happened and why. Still, the purpose of this book is to get beyond figuring out who is *good* and who is *bad* and to understand that we are all facing challenges as part of being human—challenges that, when addressed, can lead to tremendous growth and deep love.

Given the complicated feelings confronting many couples struggling with infidelity, it can be extremely difficult for both partners to not act out emotionally without first considering the consequences of their actions. Everyone is an individual. Every relationship has a unique dynamic. Yet my strongest recommendation to *all* couples—my principal overall prescription—is: *THINK BEFORE YOU ACT.* At least one person's impulsiveness is what got you into this mess. More impulsiveness will only wreak further havoc. Instead, prioritize deep reflection. Reflection is the life raft that has the power to buoy you through these rough waters and carry you to the shoreline of a healthy, happy future for you and your spouse—whether you wind up landing there together, with a newly fortified relationship, or apart, with new adventures ahead of each of you.

In Part III, I will offer recommendations on how to mend yourselves and move forward. We'll discuss emotional and sexual healing, with guidelines for each partner to follow individually as well as rules for the couple to follow together. We'll address the age-old question: Should I stay or should I go? And we'll delve into the critical issues of how and when to share with other people what's going on—most critically your children. We'll talk about how to lay the foundation for a love and sexual life that is lasting. Recovering from an affair is a Herculean effort for all involved. But I promise you: regardless of whether your relationship survives this upset, you can move into a better life than you ever imagined.

chapter 8

Discovery: The truth comes out— what now?

Twenty-two years after saying "I do," Alvin discovered that his wife, Susan, was in the midst of a yearlong affair. The couple had school-aged children. He wanted desperately to keep their marriage intact. Alvin yelled, begged, cajoled, threatened, raged, negotiated, and even enlisted Susan's friends and family to pressure her to stay. But Susan had other plans. Her desires had led her to share confidences and seek her most intimate connections with another man. This convinced her that the relationship with her husband must be over. She packed her bags and left. As she walked out the door, she told Alvin, "I love you, but I'm not *in love* with you." Alvin was incredulous. After all, he thought, most couples lose that *in-love* feeling within the first few years of marriage. He turned to Susan and said, "Not *in love* with me? Honey, after twenty-two years, it's amazing that you don't detest me!"

Surviving and Thriving After the Affair

Losing a love is no laughing matter. And although it's true that the very intense "in love" feeling does fade, generally lasting less than a year, sustaining a long-term relationship requires love and some degree of lust throughout.

Alvin could not handle the thought of being dumped. After his wife walked out, he became disoriented and confused. He seriously considered suicide. Barely able to sleep for more than a few hours, he needed medication to fight against depression and then tranquilizers to deal with his anxiety during the lonely nights. It took three months for the worst of his symptoms to disappear, but he needed a year of determined efforts in exercise, meditation, recommitting to work, and making new friends to successfully emerge from the blow, healthier than ever.

At the end of it, not only did Alvin feel better, but he also embraced life in completely new ways. How could he have wound up better off following such heartbreak? Because with hardship comes enormous growth.

By now you know I'm not exactly a Pollyannaish kind of guy. I don't make promises I can't keep. The fact is that in my line of work I don't see roses and daffodils everywhere. Actually, I see the dark side. That's my job. To peer into the darkness and help my patients accept it, manage it, and move beyond it. If you are part of a couple living in the aftermath of an affair, you have seen some difficult times too. Your boat has been rocked, and there is no going back.

Yet humans are resilient and have evolved to endure. Sometimes we function best when our backs are against the wall and we are forced to reinvent ourselves and reconfigure old relationships into more meaningful, loving, and, yes, even sexy relationships.

So here's my promise: this nightmare can be the first step of your hero's journey. If you and your partner dedicate yourselves to rebuilding your relationship, you will become stronger than ever. Infidelity is often not personal! It is the result of common human failings. Most marriages can survive an affair. And even if yours is one of the roughly 40 to 50 percent of marriages that end in divorce, you are very likely to have a good life. **You will survive and can even thrive**—as I saw happen with Alvin.

Here in Part III we will discuss how to have a happy and healthy recovery from the discovery—whether you remain together or apart.

Stop the Impulsive Actions!

Like many good Catholic boys at his parochial school, Nate earned excellent grades, was a star athlete, learned good civic values, and kept his sexual desires to himself. He believed that the purpose of marriage was to have sex. He also learned that sex was something that polite and proper people never discussed. But his urges were intense. After college he met the woman of his dreams, and they got married and had four children. Although he didn't talk about sex much, it was always on his mind. He and his wife had a very good sex life in the beginning, but after ten years it fizzled. He became interested in other women. Although he managed to keep his desires for different women a secret—and, in secret, acted on his desires with a few of them—Nate realized this was wrong. A successful dermatologist, he flirted seriously with one of his medical residents and once slept with a colleague while away at a medical convention.

Nate was thirty-five when a nurse in his practice caught his eye. He began a deep friendship with her that quickly transcended professional bounds. They texted outside of work hours, professing their great interest in each other, sharing jokes and musings, and bandying about ideas for concerts or restaurants they'd both enjoy. They quickly became emotionally involved, and in time they thought about each other more than they thought about their spouses.

Nate's emotional attachment to this nurse confused him. *If I am completely satisfied, why would I gravitate to this person?* he wondered. He interpreted his obsession with her both as a sign that she might be his soul mate and that he was falling out of love with his wife. Instead of seeing his emotional affair as a demonstration of internal issues, he saw it as a symptom of marital troubles. Then, instead of working on his relationship with his wife, he pursued his intrigue with the nurse. They had an emotional affair, which as you'll recall from Chapter 5, is often the precursor to sex.

When Nate's wife found out, she went wild.

His wife read his texts and demanded an upfront confession, immediate confrontation, and resolution despite my advice that they take their time with this one. At first Nate denied, lied, and then minimized. His wife was smart, and she wanted more and more information. Nate went into great detail, maybe even subconsciously wanting to sabotage his marriage. His wife asked for still more information. Nate, guilt-ridden about his past indiscretions, wanted desperately to confess. He told her everything. She was enraged, yet throughout it all, Nate and his wife constantly made love. They came to therapy and took a romantic vacation in a desperate attempt to use sex to bring them back together. A month after she discovered his indiscretions, Nate's wife of ten years gathered their four children around and said, "Mommy and Daddy are getting separated." With that, an emotional affair was the straw that broke the camel's back. It destroyed a marriage that, in my opinion, might have been saved.

In the following chapters we will discuss alternatives for how to deal with both past and present emotional and sexual affairs. The fact is that both Nate and his wife deserved better. Giving themselves just one month to come to terms with Nate's philandering wasn't enough. His cheating was a terrible affront to his marriage, and his wife was certainly well within her rights to seek an immediate divorce. I don't blame her for a second. Yet with proper treatment, Nate could have put an end to his philandering ways, and the couple might have rebuilt their relationship instead of tearing their family apart. With a more thoughtful and carefully orchestrated disclosure from Nate, his wife may have been able to see it all from the perspective of his recovery from cheating and, from that, found more hope for the future. I've seen plenty of couples heal the wounds of infidelity, and it seemed a shame that Nate and his wife—not to mention their children—never had the benefit of that chance.

After hearing his story, I told Nate, "Impulsivity got you into this mess. Impulsivity pushed you and your wife into premature confessions and rounding up the children. Now, it is time for the impulsivity to stop!" Although it was too little, too late to save the marriage, it was not too late to save Nate, my patient, from a future of stupid mistakes.

Jilted Spouses, It Will Be Okay!

You can prevent enormous damage to yourself and your family if you can keep yourself together. My most urgent message to you is: *Chill.* This is prescription number one. Please, if you read nothing else in this book, read this single word! Although discovering an affair most often happens by chance and the initial confrontation is usually unplanned (although some spouses leave a trail of clues and seem to want to get caught), full disclosure of and recovery from an affair should be thoughtful, planned, and carefully executed.

To get to a point where you can think clearly, you'll first need to understand what you're dealing with.

Betrayal Trauma

An estimated 90 percent of partners never find out about the cheating. For those 10 percent who do, the ramifications can be dramatic. Even for the cheater, the moment their spouse discovers their affair can be the worst moment of their lives.

A betrayed spouse often feels alone and bereft. Some of my patients have endured combat, lost loved ones, and suffered incredible challenges in life, but nothing prepared them for their spouse's betrayal. It is a terrible experience to feel rejected. That's not because their spouse was so great or the marriage was so splendid; rather, it's because the betrayal and loss have occurred outside of their control. Something indelibly human has been disrupted: the need to feel loved and securely connected, which is etched into our DNA. This means that rejection strikes at the heart of our evolutionary need to bond and our fears of being cast out of the tribe. Just as love is the strongest addiction—the most intense stimulator of the brain's reward system—losing love can plunge us into a painful withdrawal and panic.

Betrayed partners often wind up questioning themselves, their past relationships, their place in the world, and even their sense of reality. My patient Anthony explained this way how his wife felt when she discovered his obsession with porn: "a man or woman in these situations becomes temporarily insane!" People confronting their partner's infidelity may come face to face with their insecurities about whether they will ever be truly loved. They may be confronted by the existential loneliness of life and a deep unrequited desire for safety—a yearning that can be traced back to our first breath as a newborn infant when we cried out at the loss of the warmth, sustenance, comfort, and connection of the womb.

Let's discuss what I mean by *trauma*. The actual event matters little. What matters is the meaning we derive from the experience. The same event can affect different people in very different ways. The same event can even affect the *same person* differently depending on the circumstances of their life at that very moment. So trauma refers not to the event but to its psychological imprint—the scars, anxieties, self-doubts, depression, and fears etched in the brain. Depending on a host of factors, from an individual's temperament to their level of outside support, the aftereffects can last from months to years. Traumas caused by exposure to life-threatening fires, hurricanes, and explosions are tough to get over. Yet betrayal traumas can be even more damaging because you experience rejection and fear for yourself and your children.

As a betrayed spouse, you may develop a posttraumatic stress disorder (PTSD), with flashbacks, nightmares, and dissociation (meaning you feel unreal or *out of it*). You might experience signs of clinical depression, such as weight loss, depressed mood, and sleeplessness. You could have fleeting thoughts of suicide. Or you may experience a milder mental disorder called an *adjustment disorder* with anxious and/or depressive symptoms. Past mental disorders that are otherwise dormant may become active again. For example, an otherwise mild and unnoticed bipolar disorder may suddenly become so acute that you require hospitalization. Aside from your mental health, your physical health may deteriorate, and preexisting conditions like asthma and stomach problems can get much worse.

Trauma and depression change your brain architecture. As we've discussed, the brain evolved to get turned on by love, sex, novelty, and thrill. Our brains also evolved to register threatening events like the loss of family so that we never forget them. Remember we discussed how during orgasm our brains slow activity everywhere except in our pleasure centers? Likewise, during a traumatic event the brain dampens down activity in all but the fear and action centers, focusing our attention on critical functions while the fear centers assess danger and damage and then the fight-or-flight system prepares us for action.

During the trauma itself parts of the brain literally shut down in an effort toward preservation, preventing the brain from going into overdrive, like a household circuit breaker that shuts off the power to prevent a fire. The *amygdala*—the fear storage center of the brain—becomes activated along with other parts of the brain that assess danger. The release of stress chemicals put the brain on high alert. PTSD can cause the memory section of the brain, called the *hippocampus*, to decrease in volume while the amygdala is increasing. A brain sensitized in this way reacts more intensely to the stress hormones norepinephrine and cortisol. This change in the brain sets the stage for some of the behaviors a betrayed spouse might display.

PTSD? Really? Yes.

It might be difficult for people—especially a cheating spouse who's feeling defensive—to understand how an affair could cause the same stress disorder suffered by combat veterans. Some less contrite offenders might even wonder: *What's the big deal?*

Yet the fallout from events like the betrayal of a spouse linger for a long time, and the aggrieved partner often spends weeks to years trying to figure out what went wrong and who was to blame.

When people suffer through stressful events, antidepressants (which are also effective anti-anxiety medications) may help protect the brain from the temporary and possibly permanent changes resulting from chronic stress. There is some data that medications like certain blood pressure medications called *beta-blockers* may also be helpful. But what helps the most with PTSD is talking through the trauma properly and realizing that you will survive and have a chance for growth.

Common Mistakes Made by the Betrayed Spouse

If you're like most betrayed spouses, your head is spinning and you want an immediate resolution. You want to know everything, sometimes including the details of the sexual liaisons.

You may find yourself searching retrospectively for the clues that you missed. *How much did s/he lie to me? Where was s/he that night? Where was I while they were in bed together? How many were there?* Cheated-upon partners are desperate to understand. Like Lady Macbeth washing her hands until they bleed, you are trying to cleanse yourself with knowledge. You seek understanding and a renewed sense of safety. You are not just trying to retaliate; you are probably actually hoping to find nothing incriminating to reassure yourself that you can trust again. You can't get the betrayal out of your mind. Sleep is difficult. The quiet darkness of night invites images of the affair, which you may have gleaned through texts and emails or your own imagination, replaying over and over through your mind.

Common Mistakes Made by the Cheating Spouse

The cheating spouse *also* wants everything settled ASAP. If you are sincerely upset, your tears and remorse should be shared. After that, although you shouldn't expect immediate absolution, you will want resolution soon enough. Meanwhile your spouse is aghast, having learned about your actions, and no matter what you say, s/he replies that you are still lying and keeps interrogating you further. You may try to rationalize—surely there were good reasons why you cheated. At some point you might feel compelled to change your story about what led you to stray, and maybe, you think, your spouse could have been a better partner. My advice, before you rush into some combination of denial, confession, incrimination, and self-incrimination, is: *Slow down.*

Stop and think before you speak and act. Be contrite, but make sure you don't say anything you can't unsay. It may even be a sign of your honesty if you say, "I need some more time to think about how to tell this to you because I don't want to lie or manipulate anymore. Give me time to give you thoughtful answers."

As much as you would like this nightmare of discovery to be over, it may take weeks, months, maybe years, and sometimes a lifetime to unravel, explain, and understand what went down. You can't condense this process into a few conversations over a couple of hours. If you try, you do so at your own peril.

Gaslighting and the Cheating Spouse

The term *gaslighting* was popularized by the 1944 George Cukor film *Gaslight*, in which the dashing and sinister Charles Boyer tries to convince the innocent and beautiful bride Ingrid Bergman that she is losing her mind in order to steal her jewels. In the context of infidelity, *gaslighting* means that you deny and undermine your spouse's sense of reality in order to gain power in the relationship or win an argument. Gaslighting is pretty standard operating procedure for a cheating spouse who's trying to hide their philandering, and it can take many forms.

Another technique the gaslighting spouse uses is to focus their accuser on the facts of the case that are incorrect while withholding incriminating information. For, example, a cheating husband may say to his wife, "I never had sex with Susie. I never even had the slightest interest in her. You're out of your mind! You're paranoid!" Well, maybe he never had sex with Susie, but he had oral sex with Paula and kissed Jane, none of which his wife knows about. He met Celia at the airport during his last business trip, which he never told his wife either. He confided his marital problems to sexy Samantha, which his wife doesn't know. Get my point? Don't gaslight. Don't deny

Betrayed spouses, beware

You will likely find it extremely difficult not to dig for the damning and salacious details that will only make your heartache worse and inhibit your healing. This hunger is your mind's (dysfunctional) effort to understand how someone you trusted could do you so wrong. Your constant surveillance of emails, credit card bills, and so on will turn you into what I call a *surveillance monster*, searching high and low for examples of betrayal despite the fact that your efforts bring anguish to everyone, particularly yourself. Perhaps you want to memorialize your spouse's misdeeds for friends, family, or your own understanding. Or maybe even for the possible divorce lawyers. You will spend sleepless nights reviewing the records. You will sneak onto your cheating spouse's phone and computer. This activity will create a great deal of misery not just for your spouse but also yourself. In the sex-addiction literature, when betrayed spouses relentlessly seek out detailed information on the sexual acting out, it is called *pain shopping*.

If you proceed to divorce, your recordkeeping will achieve little more than lining your lawyers' pockets when they charge you for each minute spent combing through your many incriminating files. This, even though most states do not consider infidelity a crime and cheating often has little bearing on the legal or financial outcome of your divorce. Unless your spouse was exposing young children to some heinous, risky situation, infidelity will have little impact on the court's determinations.

In sum, being a relentless Sherlock Holmes on the trail of your cheating spouse has little merit and is more likely to destroy the marriage than to help it. It is also likely to interfere with your mental and physical well-being. You will probably want to review the basic facts of the cheating more than once with your partner. But try to exercise the self-control necessary to keep yourself from digging for painful details.

Cheaters, be warned

At first you will minimize your philandering behaviors. You will deny. You will hedge. You will tell quarter-truths, then half-truths. As each bit of information leaks out, you will dig yourself deeper into a hole. Your lies are likely to fail because although your spouse may never find out the whole truth, s/he will find more and more evidence. And when they catch you in yet another lie, they'll likely never again trust you, effectively ending the relationship.

If you're a cheater, you're in the habit of manipulating people. This is not a value judgment; it's just fact. Let me offer this bit of advice: your spouse is onto you now. One betrayed spouse told me, "Each little lie from him chips away at me. I'm not a starfish. I can't grow new legs. I can't undo what I've now learned about him. How can I ever trust him again?" Despite knowing it is wrong, you will be inclined to continue to manipulate.

For instance, you will be tempted to tell your accuser lies and false justifications like, "You told me it's okay if I have an affair. Don't you remember that? Remember that one time when you were so angry, you turned beet red and told me, 'We're over. Screw someone else for all I care!'" Or, "What did you expect, given how you treated me?" Or, "I wasn't looking for an affair. We were only friends, nothing more. S/he was nice to me, unlike you!" Or, "I'm not having an affair. You're just trying to control me." There may be a grain of truth in any of these justifications, but it ignores the fundamental agreement you had to be monogamous and denies your dishonest actions.

your partner's sense of reality. Not only will that approach fail, but it's also a crappy way to treat someone—especially someone to whom you've pledged your love.

The opposite of gaslighting is *empathic understanding.* This means you listen to the other person and try to take in their experience. You try to comprehend how your actions made them feel. Even though it is hard to hear the impact of your betrayal, you do not deny their sense of reality because it conflicts with your agenda. You do your best to understand what it is like to be in their shoes. Empathic understanding is a very good idea at this critical juncture in your relationship.

What Do We Tell Other People?

My prescription—*Chill!*—involves pausing before you take steps that might cause further damage. A big piece of this is thinking ahead before rushing to tell other people, including your children. If you're a betrayed spouse, you may be seeking vengeance, processing rejection, or perhaps struggling with PTSD. If you are a cheating spouse, your head will be spinning as you watch the cascade of falling dominoes. It will be nearly impossible for either of you to hide your feelings from your loved ones. So what do you tell those closest to you?

If you tell them nothing, you rob yourself of the opportunity for support and reasonable advice. If you tell everyone everything, you're inviting their intrusive involvement. As with most things regarding infidelity, there is no single, easy answer. Most therapists who deal with these matters would probably agree with this guideline: *Be discreet, and be thoughtful!*

Although it may be impossible to hide your emotions and keeping your troubles a secret may be ill advised, you need to check your motivations at every step along the way. Are you looking for support? That's good. Or are you seeking revenge? That's destructive! Are you looking to logically figure out your next steps with the support of reliable people, or are you looking for someone to help you justify your actions? Are you open to evaluating this problem from all reasonable points of view and to thoughtful input from others? Or are you just looking for someone to agree with you and fortify your own positions to support your old arguments?

Whether you're the betrayed spouse or the cheating spouse, if there was ever a time to think outside the box and be open to self-reflection, invoke the wisdom of others, and think before you speak and act, this is such a time. It is good to find an objective source of support and guidance. Clergy, licensed therapists, or even trusted family and friends can be very helpful at this point.

In asking for support, you need to safeguard the confidentiality of what you're about to share. Infidelity happens every day and to tens of millions of people and needs to be discussed openly. However, you do not want your raw, angry thoughts and statements made in the heat of the moment broadcasted to a wider audience. If you're the betrayed, avoid spreading trash talk about how big a creep your spouse is. If you're the cheater, avoid proclaiming how justified your actions were. That kind of dialogue will not help anyone. People love to tittle-tattle about other people's romantic and sexual losses to help them feel better about their own problems and conflicts. Your tale of woe may make for great gossip in your community, but how can that be helpful in the long run?

Similarly, creating a negative media campaign against your spouse will further polarize you and is likely to backfire. Divorce your spouse if you want, but creating a battlefield with opposing troops cannot help you, your relationship, or your children.

Which brings us to the most critical issue for many readers: what to tell the children.

Healing the Family and What to Tell the Kids

Unfortunately, the secret of infidelity is often known to the children even when the cheated-upon spouse is in the dark. Frequently the children are aware of the affair(s) and retain the memory in their unconscious. Sometimes, when children uncover the truth, the cheating parent tells them, "Keep the secret between us. Mom/Dad just wouldn't understand." In this way children of all ages are turned into coconspirators and are forced to form ambivalent relationships and alliances in the family. Because cheating is so common and kids tend to be so aware, many children carry this kind of awful secret and live in an atmosphere of silent distrust and shame.

Children may seem fine with the infidelity. That's because children are resilient—until they aren't. Young kids, under the age of about ten, tend to talk openly about their problems. But even after the crying stops, the effects of such family dishonesty and decay will stay with them for a lifetime. Preteens and teens appear to be good at ignoring and tuning out, only to have their inner distress result in poor grades, early sex, and alcohol and drug use down the road. Conversely, older teens and adult children often respond with a mixture of dismissiveness (e.g., "You guys are crazy. This has nothing to with me.") and rage (e.g., "How could you cheat?!?"). They can be very judgmental and see sexual transgressions as an affront to the entire family and a violation of the sanctity of the home. Or they can retreat to their room, burying themselves in their video games and phone.

On the issue of what to tell the children, one of the world's experts on disclosure in matters of sexual transgressions and addiction is family therapist Dr. Stephanie Carnes, daughter of my mentor Dr. Patrick Carnes and editor of *Mending the Shattered Heart: A Guide for Partners of Sex Addicts*. She advises that the guiding principle must be what's in the children's best interest. If the kids are unaware of what's going on, it's best to protect them from the knowledge. But in cases in which the parents are falling apart or in obvious distress, providing the children with some explanation is crucial. Otherwise, without some basic information, children may wind up making up stories in their heads about what's wrong that are often worse than the reality.

Critical to deciding what information to share are considerations for what's developmentally appropriate for your child. For young children she suggests that it might be appropriate to say something along the lines of: "Daddy lied to Mommy, so Mommy's very upset. But this has nothing to do with you. Mommy and Daddy are working on it, and you don't need to worry about it." Another option, again, depending on the child's age and level of understanding, might be something like, "Mommy had a boyfriend. Mommy's not supposed to have a boyfriend. Daddy's supposed to be Mommy's only boyfriend. So now Mommy's not in that relationship anymore. Mommy and Daddy are not getting divorced." To many parents and experts alike, this can seem like way too much information. No expert can tell you exactly what to say or how to be a good parent to your particular kids during this time of turmoil. But the overall principle is clear: minimize the damage to your children.

Betrayed spouses are angry and traumatized. They often seek revenge. They may unconsciously and unknowingly involve their children in seeking revenge. You may feel that the child should know immediately that this was bad behavior and your spouse is not to be trusted. Perhaps that's true, but you'll have a lifetime to speak to them about it. Once you let the cat out of the bag, however, your children will never forget your words—that I promise.

It is the norm, I'm sorry to say, for even the best-intended and most altruistic parents to say hurtful things. Be careful. If you tell your child something bad about their other parent, more often than not the child unconsciously hears it as something bad about themselves. Children identify with their parents, even those whom they believe to be the "bad" or "crazy" parent. An insult against any parent is often interpreted by the child as somehow revealing the child's own defects. Then there's the issue of which parent the child defends.

Dr. Stephanie Carnes also cautions against saying or doing anything that puts a child into the position of having to take sides. "You always want to give the child permission to love the other parent," she says. "The betrayed partner might *feel* like wanting to tell the kid everything, but it's never in the child's best interest to damage the relationship with their other parent." In addition, children will sometimes unconsciously learn the bad behavior. If they are traumatized, they often repeat that which upsets them.

Remember: the damage the affair has done to you and your family may be terrible. But the last thing you want to do while in the wake of this affair and possibly on the brink of divorce is to traumatize your children or have them go through pain that in any way approaches your own suffering.

chapter 9

Disclosure: Prepare yourself for the messiness

During conversations between cheating and cheated-upon partners there is an automatic imbalance of emotions, and neither party can truly understand the others' attitudes. I am telling you this now because I don't want you to expect something different. This may be hard to wrap your head around, but here goes: often the cheating spouse may have little genuine remorse. Yes, you read that correctly. More than a few cheating spouses inwardly and sometimes even outwardly gloat, full of pride over being desirable and having conquered a new lover. Sounds terrible, I know, but

I've seen it time and time again. Even if the cheater feels re-morse, their first reaction is not anything that approaches the terrible pain of rejection and humiliation the cheated-upon spouse experiences, so the dialogue between them never feels equal in terms of pain and anguish.

Here's one more thing that happens surprisingly often in the dynamic between the spouses. The rejected spouse often wants their partner even more. How crazy is that? Somehow, unconsciously, the rejected partner feels that if they can win their spouse back, they will be validated. Because we hate to lose love, we often do stupid things to prevent that from hap-pening. So the cheating spouse suddenly seems extra desir-able, and the jilted spouse feels that they have something to prove to get their spouse back. This is a recipe for disaster.

To make matters worse, the spouse who was once a source of comfort is now the source of pain. Before, when you felt wronged by someone, lied to, you used to run to your spouse for solace, seeking refuge in your relationship. But what hap-pens when your trusted confidante and the perpetrator are one and the same? When the person who usually consoles you is the one responsible for your despair? What a mess!

Disclosure

Discovery describes the moment when a betrayed partner finds out about their spouse's affair, but *disclosure* is when they really learn what happened. Sometimes people feel so certain about how to proceed that they can't help but rush into a full disclo-sure, often followed by an immediate reconciliation or pro-ceeding to bitter divorce. Although nearly everyone wants im-mediate answers as soon as infidelity comes to light, I say: take a breath before you say too much. The human mind takes a while to wrap itself around a radically new set of circumstances.

With compulsive cheaters, therapists usually plan a careful disclosure over the course of weeks to months while both spouses enter therapy. After each spouse works through their individual questions and answers, the spouses come together with a separate couple's therapist in order to address and answer all the questions about the affair(s).

Sounds good, but unfortunately, that's an impractical scenario for most people. Most couples don't have the time, money, patience, or access to an army of therapists who can sit in a room with them for months to hash things out. Therefore, as most people will take it upon themselves to resolve the affair, here are some steps to follow during disclosure.

When Discussing the Affair, Seek Understanding, Not Pain

Most people want to know some, if not all of the romantic and sexual details. Although that desire is normal and understandable, demanding that information leads to more harm than good. If you're a betrayed spouse, you should know generally what happened, how it happened, how many times it happened, where it happened, and generally whom it happened with.

When it comes to sharing details, Dr. Stephanie Carnes holds to the general rule that a betrayed partner should be given "clear factual information that doesn't leave the partner guessing, that empowers them with the truth, and gives them the ability to make positive choices for themselves." What shouldn't be provided is unnecessary information, including "pictures or images" that provide "fodder for rumination" that feeds into PTSD. "Specific sex acts, or where they went for dinner, or what they were wearing, or what hotels they stayed at—that is usually not helpful," she says. If you insist on discussing sex, use proper anatomical terms ("penis" vs. "cock") and noncurse words (e.g., "We had sexual intercourse." vs. "We fucked.").

Inevitably a betrayed spouse will ask: "Do you love him/her?," "Was the sex better with him/her?," and the perennial "Why did you do it?" These questions are often unanswerable. Love is a complex and fickle feeling. You may seek out sex for reasons you never fully understand. You can love someone one moment and feel relatively disinterested the next. Many of my patients promised their affair partners that they would marry them, feeling that genuine desire in the heat of the romance yet never coming close to keeping that promise. Was the sex better? Most often the sex was better. "Why did you do it?" It might take years of therapy to adequately answer the "why" question.

Unfaithful partners should give these questions and answers some careful consideration, write them down, and then address them in a calm fashion. As much as possible, stick to the basics and answer any answerable questions. The details are likely to be hurtful and haunting to your spouse.

But the reality is—and I can't stress this enough—that the betrayed spouse will probably *never* know everything. In my experience, with the best of intentions, cheating spouses often leave out details for fear of hurting their loved ones and destroying their own lives.

To get to the truth, some experts actually advise using polygraph tests! You know, those electronic tests you see in cop shows in which the accused undergoes questioning with electrodes attached to their skin. The skin test assesses the nervousness of the person being questioned, which *may* indicate lying. But polygraphs are so unreliable that they are inadmissible in most courts. Besides, do you really want to decide whether you should remain married to a cheating spouse on the basis of a semireliable skin test? Moreover, once you begin questioning your spouse with polygraph testing, you don't have a romantic partner anymore but rather a prisoner subject to periodic interrogation.

What everyone *does* need to know is whether there's a possibility of the cheating spouse picked up any sexually transmitted diseases (STDs). If you decide to have sex immediately after the discovery of infidelity (which I advise against—more on this in Chapter 11), you should use condoms for protection for a period of at least three months after your spouse pledges fidelity or until you have further facts about what happened sexually and a discussion with your doctor about your personal risk of STDs. (Keep in mind that oral sex comes with risks for STDs as well.)

After sexual transgression I advise that both partners get tested for a variety of sexually transmitted diseases, including HIV (the virus that causes AIDS), herpes, chlamydia, gonorrhea, and syphilis, among others. Many clinics have a standard panel of STD tests. Women should also have a gynecological exam, including a Pap smear to see if they have been infected with HPV, a virus that can cause warts and cancers. Some STDs may not be detected for an extended period, so both partners should be retested repeatedly for up to one year. Some illnesses, like HPV among men, cannot be readily detected, and some tests are not definitive for people who are carriers of sexually transmitted viruses. However, something serious like HIV is easily and definitively detected.

For the Cheating Spouse:
How to Deal with Your Affair Partner

Ah, and what about the affair partner? That sex playmate to whom you may have even confessed your love. Before you dump them, you need to do some soul searching. If you decide this person belongs in your life and is an appropriate sex and/or romantic partner for the short or long term, by all means, I encourage you to find a way to *honestly* keep your affair partner close to you. No doubt there were compelling reasons why you got together in the first place. The relationship surely provided something you felt you desperately wanted, such as sex, love, companionship, excitement, escape—maybe all the above. This person has captured your reward center.

However, in sexual compulsivity terms, a person who ignites your reward system in a dysfunctional relationship may be called a *qualifier*—in other words, the person who qualifies you as being locked in an unhealthy relationship with sex and love. And of course such a person or situation has no place in a healthy life.

And if your partner is a qualifier? Think about it this way: if your once-drug-addicted child finally got clean, you would insist that they terminate any kind of relationship with their drug dealer out of fear that contact could trigger a relapse, right? This situation is no different. Old sex partners are tempting. But if you want your marriage to continue, you must demonstrate your unequivocal and primary dedication to your life partner.

Even if spouses ultimately decide to have an open, nonmonogamous marriage, the clandestine affair partner may be too toxic a force to be permitted into the couple's life. Certainly they have already demonstrated disrespect for the marital rules. Hence, you will probably need to respectfully and without ambiguity disavow, disengage, and disentangle from the affair partner. Very hard to do!

Disengaging can be very delicate. Not only do you have yearnings and feelings for them, but you may also fear that the jilted affair partner will seek revenge by going to your employer, blackmail you, or try to further destroy you or your family. Jilted lovers are subject to the same rage and feelings of rejection as everyone else. So you must be thoughtful about how to reckon with a past affair partner in a respectful way that doesn't harm you, them, or your family.

Lessons Learned

Let's return to Alvin and his wife. If you recall, Alvin felt dependent and wanted to keep his wife in the marriage, while his wife, Susan, sought independence. Their psychological issues collided. This is not an insignificant issue. Throughout this book we've tackled the question, "Why do people cheat?" Well, the answer obviously has quite a bit to do with biology and evolution and with how easily human beings lie. Alvin and his wife also demonstrate how one's psychology affects why people cheat. She felt like a prisoner in the relationship. He felt dependent and was panic stricken when facing having to give up the marriage. His neediness made her more resolute.

Gender roles also affected how Alvin and his wife dealt with the discovery. Men tend to be reluctant to end a relationship unless they have another partner waiting for them, except in cases where they're married to a very destructive spouse.

Today women initiate 70 percent of divorces, although men are just as likely to end nonmarital relationships. At least one

Addiction: Concepts to keep in mind
to resist an affair partner

Here are three principles that I've borrowed from the world of treating addictions for dealing with the affair partner if you are planning on staying married and monogamous. First and foremost, *dissolution is the solution.* This means that the relationship with the affair partner often needs to end in order for you move forward with your marriage. Secondly you need to *surrender your war on reality,* in this case, surrendering your assault on the realities of being involved with your affair partner. I first heard this phrase from Wayne Zespry during a lecture about recovery from drug and alcohol addiction, but I find it to be really helpful for recovering from infidelity too. What many adulterers find in the aftermath of disclosure is that their solution (the affair) is far worse than their problem (desire for novelty, boredom, needing ego gratification, etc.). We often think an affair can liberate us and bring us some kind of nirvana. We romanticize the other man or woman, fantasizing about the wonderful possibilities in the way we might idealize alcohol, cocaine, or heroin—thinking only of the high and not the inevitable lows. In fact, our "solution" often brings a whole lot of pain, humiliation, and destruction to our lives. We need to surrender the affair and take responsibility for our behaviors and our

survey claims that among college-educated women, the wife initiates over 90 percent of the divorces. There are many reasons why women file for divorce more often than men. With regard to infidelity, many men can stick around for a lifetime, especially if they feel that staying grants them license to have extramarital sexual trysts. Suffice it to say that men tend to be reluctant to end a marriage—except when they're launching straight into another relationship. Alvin had no partner lined reality instead of living a lie. Only by accepting life on life's terms (to borrow a phrase from the addiction literature) can we experience a true, sustained, and sustaining love.

Thus far you have been thinking of your affair partner with *euphoric recall*. You've been thinking about the bliss, the escape, the embrace, the intensity of the orgasm. But don't stop there. Think the whole situation through to its realistic conclusions. How do you feel after the sex is over? What does it feel like to live a lie? Why hasn't the relationship progressed as you wanted? Doing this means you will need to abandon your fantasy-based way of looking at the affair and surrender to a more realistic appraisal.

The third principle is to *go with your values, not your feelings*. I first heard this from my colleague Martin Sherry, an addiction specialist in Manhattan. For my patients trying to abstain and recover from an addiction, it meant following their feelings and cravings that led them to drink or eat too much. "Feelings tend to be conflicted. Feelings tend to be fleeting. Once I clarify what my values are," Marty explains, "it is easier to be proactive as opposed to simply being reactive to events and people/systems." So if you have a history of repeatedly violating your values in favor of your desires for sex, focusing on your true mores and priorities in life can help ward off temptation.

up and was determined to keep his wife. Her rejection severely wounded his ego, and he could not contain his anger, to the point that Susan felt unsafe with him.

After Alvin and Susan divorced, he began therapy and ended up happy. But before treatment Alvin's fears of abandonment and Susan's sense of imprisonment caused them both to proceed impulsively and emotionally at their children's expense. Alvin was freaking out. Susan moved out, leaving

---

For the betrayed spouse:
How to deal with the affair partner

Even though trust was broken, there are boundaries that need to be respected. If the affair partner was a close friend or a relative, you should *probably* know their name(s). Otherwise, even if the affair partner acted like a dirty, low-down scoundrel, their privacy still needs to be protected, so it may not be wise to insist upon knowing who they are.

As the betrayed spouse, you might want to give the affair partner a piece of your mind. You may want to talk to their family or their spouse. You may want to call the affair partner or go to their home to tell them to leave your man or woman alone! Maybe you'll even want to kill them. (More than one homicide has been attributed to a vengeful spouse.) Or you may want to call them and say, "Take the asshole—he's yours!" (with a few other choice expletives). That attitude of "take him, he's yours" may actually not be such a bad attitude for you to have when dealing with your spouse at this point. But in general, and with few exceptions, the less contact you have with the affair partner, the better off you will be.

---

him in the house with the children. With the family in conflict, the children's formerly outstanding school performances deteriorated, which ultimately affected their college choices. Everyone's health suffered. The kids began staying out to avoid the chaos in their home and wound up reining in their lofty career dreams. Although the children were resilient enough to ultimately rise above the turmoil of their parents' breakup through deep psychotherapy work, the fact remained that the rash decisions their parents made in the heat of an ugly moment wound up having lifelong repercussions for them.

If you are the betrayed spouse, then just spotting the affair partner in the neighborhood, let alone engaged with your spouse or family on an ongoing basis, will likely infuriate you. Many affair partners are people known to the couple and may even be your friends or relatives. In these cases it may not be practical or desirable to exile them. Here you will need to swallow your pride to do what is best for yourself and your family. Try your best to forgive the affair partner for their transgressions with some assurance that they will no longer secretly engage with your spouse.

Don't blame the affair on the affair partner. To put the responsibility on the affair partner may be convenient, but it is untrue. Confronting the affair partner may give you a false sense of confidence, a false belief that you have solved the problem and gotten rid of the competition. Sorry, so far from the reality. The problem was never with the "competition" or the affair partner; the problem was—and is—with your spouse. Contacting all the potential partners in your neighborhood won't help and will just create an aura of insanity.

Here's a different disclosure situation that was managed better: Vicky had no children. She was a teacher in the public school system. She had been in my addiction group therapy to deal with her recovery from alcoholism and had remained sober for six years. Like many people who find that with sobriety comes new awareness of other troubles, Vicky recognized problems in her marriage and needed to talk through them. This common scenario is why I always recommend concurrent couple's therapy if one partner is working to overcome an addiction. When people get sober and no longer have substances to shield them, they often find themselves confronting new, stark views of their lives.

In group it became apparent that Vicky had been ignoring the signs of a cheating husband. He'd spent years in Asia for work as a construction engineer, and they hadn't had sex in three years. These realities had "affair" written all over them. However, it wasn't until his twenty-two-year-old girlfriend called Vicky from mainland China and told her that she wanted to marry Vicky's husband that she could no longer hide her head in the sand. The phone call caused Vicky to fall into classic reactive depression with PTSD. She had no appetite, couldn't concentrate, and had sleepless nights with intrusive thoughts and plots of revenge.

Fortunately Vicky reentered intensive therapy and started a low dose of a mild antidepressant to help her manage her emotions. In talk therapy she began to recognize the problems that had plagued her marriage for years, evidenced by the lack of emotional and sexual intimacy between her and her husband. Vicky realized her husband also needed psychological help and insisted that he get it if he wanted her to stay. He agreed to disavow himself of his affair partner, implored Vicky to stay with him, and agreed to work on the relationship. (More about Vicky a little later.)

Meanwhile here's one more example of how things went right in a family with four preteen children: Tina lost it when she found scores of email messages that her husband had exchanged with prostitutes. This paragon of virtue in the community, at their church, as a foreman on the job, and among their friends had been living a lie. The possibility that he would cheat had never occurred to Tina. In fact, cheating had never crossed her husband's mind either. Instead, he so completely compartmentalized his infidelity that he justified having sex with scores of prostitutes within just a few years by telling himself, "It's just sex. It means nothing. It's just what guys do."

But when Tina found out, her world, her very reality, crumbled. Distraught, she exhibited all the symptoms of PTSD. Yet Tina was determined to keep her feelings from destroying herself and her children, whom she protected from the information. Tina gathered the data she needed to slowly but surely evaluate her marriage. Her husband was contrite and showed remorse, but as I say, cheating spouses tend to inwardly feel almost proud of their extramarital sex quests and almost never feel the deep pain of the person who is betrayed. Not uncommonly, the cheating spouse even has a hint of a smirk on his or her face. As a doctor, I have to say that it is rather painful for me to watch a betrayed spouse undergoing severe trauma, discussing the pain of discovering the affair, all while sitting next to a cheating spouse wearing a slight smirk. But I've seen it enough times to know it's not personal; it's just a manifestation of some of the worst aspects of human nature. It may also have to do with the fact that infidelity can often be an act of aggression or revenge against the betrayed spouse. (Of course, none of this is anything that most cheating spouses are aware of. These actions occur on a largely unconscious basis.)

Even as Tina's cheating husband initially continued to rationalize his cheating as "normal guy behavior" and compartmentalized his whoring as unrelated to his integrity, Tina remained focused not on her husband becoming a better person but on how she and her family could survive and thrive. Tina saw a therapist in my practice for support and sent her husband to me. I worked to break his denial. Her husband told me a story that I have heard over and over—that the first time he went to a prostitute he felt like a heel. But after he saw the prostitutes again and again, he was amazed at how easy it was to cheat

on his wife. This caring, generally concerned, and socially responsible man conveniently ignored the fact that many of the
prostitutes he hired from brothels in New York had been taken
from their rural third-world homes as young girls and forced
into prostitution. His deceiving mind had managed to keep
the truth at bay.

In therapy, however, we face up to our truths. When I confronted him with his lies and he had to look at them over and
over, he couldn't believe the illicit and immoral behavior he
had fallen into. Like many men who receive intensive treatment, he ultimately fully and honestly disclosed everything to
his wife at her request. The couple did well, their marriage
survived, and the children's upbringing was not interrupted.

Manage Your Anger and Focus on Your Health

Allow me to digress for a moment. There is little dispute that
one of the greatest athletes in history was boxer Muhammad
Ali. His boxing strategy was to disable his opponent. Before
any punches were ever thrown in the ring, in public interviews,
at a press conference, or when the referee would read the rules
at the start of match, Ali would taunt his opponent with a ti-
rade of humiliating insults. Ali, himself a humanitarian and a
civil rights advocate, went as far as hurling racial slurs against
his African American opponents simply to rattle them.

What's my point? Anger is destructive! When we are angry
and upset, we lose our higher functioning (remember the discussion of how the traumatized brain works), we lose track of
intentions, we may doubt ourselves, and we forget our strategy.
The surest way to lose in life and love might be to allow anger
to drive us. The greatest fighter in the history of boxing knew
that.

From the first moments after discovering their husbands'
philandering, Vicky and Tina were determined to survive and

thrive by keeping their emotions in check. Although Alvin had good intentions, he lacked the understanding of what was happening to him; instead, his jilted brain was running the show.

Shouldn't we, like Alvin, always try to hang onto the relationship and fight to keep the family together? Yes, but only to a point. People worry that they need to cling to their partners for dear life. What they ought to worry about, in my opinion, is strategizing for the success of their lives, their families, and their future. In my experience jilted spouses who are willing to lose a relationship are actually more likely to keep it. That is one of the ironies of relationships: if you hold onto a long-term relationship as though your life depends on it, chances are you'll either hold onto an overly dependent, unhealthy connection or you'll lose the relationship altogether because of your intense neediness and anger.

That's why my number-one rule for recovering from the discovery and disclosure of infidelity is to *chill*. The affair was bad enough, but how you behave in the aftermath can ruin your lives and—if you have them—your children's lives forever.

How Long Will This Hurt?

In cases in which a spouse having an affair for the first time is contrite, honestly answers all questions, makes heartfelt and sincere amends, and abandons the affair partner, a speedier resolution is possible. If the aggrieved partner is open to reconciliation and forgiveness after a due diligence period, that's a good sign. But there is no telling on how long a wronged spouse will take to heal. There is no statute of limitations on their hurt and anger.

If you rush reconciliation, you will fail and likely fall into some attempt at resolution that is half-baked and harmful. In

Cheating may be a sign that you need to move on

Life after the affair doesn't always work out happily ever after. But sometimes it can work out for the best. Even when an affair ends a marriage, it can nonetheless be the catalyst that allows couples to begin anew with separate lives.

Joan never intended to cheat. She had been faithful to her husband, her first lover, for twenty years, having sex with him twice a week but never experiencing passion. Although they had raised a family together, they shared few deep, emotional secrets. Joan kept her head down and dedicated herself to her kids and her productive career. During their second decade of marriage the couple stopped having sex, despite Joan's attempts to maintain a sex life. She never complained and only occasionally, while alone, broke into tears about what she might be missing. Then, one day, a handsome, older, married business colleague propositioned her. He could offer neither love nor any sort of relationship beyond sex. At first she was taken aback. Then, gradually, she thought more about his offer and, finally, accepted.

fact, if you're expecting to quickly settle emotional matters, you probably aren't prepared for the work that a mature, long-term relationship requires.

First, there may be a period of mourning during which the couple grieves over their loss of innocence. They can no longer lay claim to a faithful love between two pure hearts and clean souls. The promise of "I love you and want no one else" is lost. Realizing each other's humanity and seeing one another's hurtful, human flaws can cause great disappointment.

The partner who pinned hopes on fidelity is crestfallen and mourns being thrust out of Eden. Meanwhile the adulterer

Every month or two, over the course of a year, they met for long lovemaking sessions focused on a single goal: to give Joan pleasure. At long last, for the first time in her life, Joan orgasmed. From that point forward she orgasmed at every rendezvous with her new lover. By the third year of their affair Joan had become the love of the man's life. This affair had opened for Joan a door into love, passion, and intimacy. Once she saw what she had been missing all these years, there was no going back.

Determined to find a better life, Joan stopped the affair and entered individual and couple's therapy, where she realized that she and her husband of twenty years were wrong for each other. After her marriage ended, Joan found an available single man capable of emotion and passion, and they've remained in love together ever since. Her ex-husband has also done well after their divorce.

Although I cannot condone the affair and I hasten to add that only after Joan entered treatment and stopped the affair was she able to transform her confusion into meaningful change, I must recognize that for Joan and her ex-husband, the affair paved the way for each of them to open up new chapters in their lives.

may silently mourn the loss of their extramarital tryst(s) and, now more than ever, long for escape from what they may experience as a stifling marriage. The worst of it will last for a few weeks to months. As I mentioned earlier, certainly within the year, with good intentions and good behavior, many people are in a much better place. In the next chapters I'll talk about how to constructively approach emotional and sexual reconciliation if you decide to stay together, at least for the time being.

chapter 10

Emotional healing

S ex and love, the physical and emotional, are not easily separated. However, in order to zero in on each element of healing from an affair, I will divide our healing discussion into two sequential parts. First comes the emotional healing stage. Second, sexual healing.

In the emotional healing stage you now face the formidable task of figuring out what comes next. How will you each, as individuals, move forward? Will your primary relationship survive? What will happen to the affair? Do we stay or leave?

One thing that's clear in the aftermath of discovering infidelity is that hiding under a rock—as tempting as that may be—will not help. The betrayed spouse is often caught in the trap of denial or wishful thinking, hoping the affair will just fizzle out or go away without any further discussion. So let me say this as plainly as I can: if your unfaithful partner, once caught, is not 100 percent invested in stopping a blossoming affair from being consummated; or 100 percent intent on ending an existing affair; or 100 percent committed to ending their visits to prostitutes, sexual massage parlors, or other sex services—whichever the case may be—the cheating is not likely to end just because you discovered it.

If you're the spouse who has been betrayed, this is not what you were hoping to hear. But it is, based on my clinical experience as well as that of other leading relationship experts, the unfortunate reality. That's not to say that affairs don't fizzle out. Like any relationships, they do. And often, as we've seen over and over again in previous chapters, cheating spouses do come to their senses. But it's important to recognize that affairs often run their course, ending in their own way or on their own timetable. The truth may be hard to swallow, but it's rarely as simple as you catching your spouse engaging in an affair and then the affair is over.

As a betrayed spouse, you may be fine with a "don't ask, don't tell" policy. You might prefer not to know that the affair is continuing. How you choose to live your life is your own business, and no one should dictate how you respond to discovering your spouse's infidelity. Regardless, I want you to know that stopping affairs requires a committed effort on the part of the cheating spouse.

Okay, so now I've made it clear that the betrayed spouse is in quite a quandary. You have uncovered an affair. You know from reading this book that cheating spouses rarely tell the full unvarnished truth about what happened, even when caught.

And unless your cheating spouse is extremely remorseful and demonstrates strong intentions to end the extramarital trysts, the affairs won't just go away. So given all this, what's a betrayed spouse to do?

Focus on Yourself and Your Health

According to relationship therapist Patricia Love, EdD (yes, that is her name!), people dealing with an unfaithful spouse must focus on their own healing and being (or becoming) a healthy, happy person regardless of their partner. In most of the married couples Dr. Love treats, it's the husband who has strayed. She finds that some wives feeling jilted by their straying husbands try to act sexier to try to win back their man. She advises against this approach, however, cautioning that research shows that when wives act "sexier" following the disclosure of an affair, it actually "increases distaste for the wife" as well as increasing "hot, passionate feelings for the lover." Acting "sexier," she says, actually works *against* a wife getting her cheating husband back.

Instead, Dr. Love urges the spurned wife to "differentiate, to grow herself up, to get stronger." She explains that "You've got to get yourself centered—to come into your own." The goal here is not to save the marriage but rather yourself. What's more, this approach also happens to be the best way to increase the chances that your relationship will survive. The more upset, crying, and anxious a cheated-on wife acts, the guiltier the cheater will feel. Perversely, that guilt will drive him to seek escape in the affair even more. Instead, the attitude that Dr. Love suggests embracing is: "Let me show you what a good thing this is." The betrayed spouse needs to say, "This is not going to break me." Instead she needs to explore her own agendas and desires, following her own dreams about what she wants to do and who she wants to be. Dr. Love wisely advises the betrayed spouse to embark on endeavors they have been wanting to pursue, like starting that new business, writing that book, or taking that class. As I've said before, betrayed spouses can survive and even thrive, but it takes work.

The shame and humiliation betrayed spouses experience is often their biggest obstacle when dealing with their own lives. They usually feel devastated and sometimes embarrassed, as if what happened is somehow a reflection of their own lack of desirability. They may even shy away from friends and family. Their shame about being fooled, combined with the misperception that their cheating spouse is the *only* problem, often keeps betrayed spouses from getting the help and engaging in the self-reflection they desperately need. My patient Vicky, however, is an exception to that rule.

What Happened to Vicky?

Growth, love, reconciliation—these are not linear processes. They come with many bumps and dips in the road. Vicky, who learned through a phone call that her husband had a girlfriend overseas, worked very hard to figure out how to deal with him. She was determined not to let the revelation destroy her, but her journey was not without suffering. Initially her contrite husband begged for forgiveness and promised to drop the girlfriend and do whatever it takes to get the marriage back on track, including therapy to deal with his history of lying to her and leading a double-life with a twenty-two-year-old who expected to marry him. Before long, though, he changed his tune.

Not long after the disclosure of the affair, Vicky learned that her husband would be going back to live in Asia for business, with no definite plans about when we would return to the States. He wound up declining therapy, saying what many spouses say: that he only needed to talk to his wife about this, not to some shrink. Before he moved back, the couple scheduled a stay-at-home vacation, where he expected all would be forgiven and they would have sex and go on with life. Vicky, however, was not ready to have sex immediately. She wanted to work on the relationship first—thoughtfully and with good intentions.

Without a doubt, her husband's backpedaling and trying to get things back to "normal" without investing time into healing the relationship was a bad sign for the future of the marriage. Vicky didn't want to rush into divorce or make any hasty decision about her future, but she no longer wanted to pretend all was well. She told me, "I made a decision to not make a decision—for now."

There was no getting around it. She had come face to face with the potential destruction of her two-decades-long marriage. I explained to her that whether she liked it or not or approved or not, married businessmen working overseas sometimes had girlfriends, and there could be dozens of prostitutes in the lobbies of the major hotels that businessmen frequented. She came to realize that her husband liked Asia for the sexual opportunities. And although he promised fidelity, there was no way to ensure his faithfulness. She had no intentions of trying to spy on him. Not only would it prove impossible, but it would also divert her attention from healing and making herself strong and whole.

Despite her PTSD, characterized by mental anguish during the day and sleeplessness and feeling ill at ease at night, she was brave and kept up a good front at work. Vicky was hurting, so I prescribed an antidepressant to help ease her difficulty with concentrating, struggle with maintaining focus at her job, anxiety, irritability, trouble falling asleep, and feeling down in the dumps—all signs of depression.

Vicky was determined to make herself as healthy as possible. As her therapist, I worked to help her survive and thrive. I told her that trying to make the marriage work was a good idea but that pleading with him to stay or behave and focusing on policing him might only empower his philandering. We talked about how she would remain open to love and a lasting relationship with her husband. At the same time I recommended a good lawyer to help her prepare for a bad outcome, dealing with finances and divorce proceedings.

Most importantly, though, Vicky became committed to "doing her"—to saving herself. Vicky wanted to become a better, more sexual, more alive person, with or without her husband. She and her husband hadn't had sex in three years, and she had become completely asexual, not even masturbating in all that time. I advised her to buy a vibrator and start thinking about sex. I suggested she wear sexy undergarments. I wanted Vicky to feel sexy all day long and think about sex and joy. With her new sex toy, for the first time in three years, Vicky had an orgasm. In fact, she had three orgasms. Vicky had a new sense of self and she was on the road to recovery.

The Need for Self-Examination

After significant life events, including the disclosure of an affair, people usually ask themselves soul-searching questions, often starting with: *What is love?* When patients admit to me that they've cheated without giving it a second thought, many wonder if they even know what love is. Unfaithful spouses assume they must not love their spouses if they could so easily cheat on them. Who and how their partner is may have some bearing on infidelity, in some cases, but in *all* cases infidelity begins with the cheater—their psychology. Therefore, for the cheating spouse and betrayed spouse alike, self-examination is a critical step in the road toward recovery.

Dr. Patrick Carnes says that in the aftermath of discovering an affair, partners should take some time to evaluate their relationship. Questions to ask oneself include:

> Can I be most myself in your presence? Can I be creative, funny, vulnerable, productive, strong, weak, flamboyant, shy, or even smart? Can I couple any of those words with sex and romance? Can I be tough, forgiving, generous, spiritual, intuitive, graceful, clumsy, lazy, self-indulgent, and disciplined? Do I feel equal, successful, attractive, encouraged, trusted, and believed? Can I be fully as competent as I can be and not have my partner disappear? Do I feel challenged? Can I be accountable and hold my partner accountable? Is it okay to make a mistake? Does our time together really seem to matter?

Dr. Carnes's questions are thought provoking, all of them helping to provide the perspective and insight necessary to answer the biggest, most complex question that many couples find themselves asking in the aftermath of infidelity: *Should I stay or should I go?*

He explains the dilemma this way: "There are two decisions on the table. The first is the choice to be in a relationship. A committed relationship is a way of life that requires much of the partners. And it has little to do with whom you are with. This commitment has more to do with how much you have grown up, learned skills, developed integrity, understood your own limits, and healed your wounds. . . . The second choice is to whom you are willing to commit."

Psychologist Dr. Erich Fromm echoed that sentiment: "If love were only a feeling, there would be no basis for the promise to love each other forever. A feeling comes and it may go. Love isn't something natural. Rather it requires discipline, concentration, patience, faith, and the overcoming of narcissism. It isn't a feeling, it is a practice. . . . Love is a decision; it is a judgment; it is a promise." What Fromm is saying here is: love takes work!

Dr. Stephanie Carnes has a few questions of her own to recommend. The only way to restore trust in a relationship, she says, is "reliable behavior over time." She suggests that betrayed spouses use the following questions about their unfaithful partners to assess whether the relationship has a future: "Are they remorseful? Are they holding themselves accountable? Are their actions changing? Are their actions not matching up with their words? Are they where they say they're going to be?" She recommends that betrayed spouses hold off on making any immediate decision and instead sit back, reflect, and collect data. Ultimately, if their partner is a philanderer who does not respond to disclosure of infidelity with openness, accountability, and transparency, it's really hard for the cheated-upon partner to hold out hope for the relationship to continue.

The cheating spouse also needs to seriously answer the most important question of all: *Do I love my partner enough to stay?* Even if you decide to go, keep in mind that if you want any long-term relationship in the future, you need to decide to do the personal work required to make sure the common cycle of infatuation followed by deceit doesn't repeat again and again with this or any other partner.

Does the Cheater Need to Tell
Their Betrayed Spouse Everything?

This is a hard question. Once your affair has been uncovered, although you should avoid revealing painful details, the answer is yes—tell all, *within reason.*

Let's start with a very difficult scenario: What if your spouse has no idea you've cheated? What if the affair ended long go, and you have no intention of doing it ever again? In a perfect world I would say you should tell your spouse everything here too. Honesty begets intimacy, which creates love. However, in the imperfect world of long-term relationships, my clinical experience suggests you disclose in a very thoughtful way.

Despite my own bias toward honesty, I can't think of a single situation in my practice in which a spouse revealed an unknown secret affair to a completely unsuspecting partner that did not end up severely compromising their long-term relationship, as betrayed spouses find it very hard to hear anything that may clash with their expectations.

I can think of many such scenarios. To name a few: I treated a man who went for a massage but *wanted* to be masturbated at the end of it. He didn't get that *happy ending* but he told his wife of his desire. She immediately divorced him. I treated another man married to a woman but who'd secretly been having sex with men. He volunteered that information, and divorced soon followed. Another man, on his deathbed, told his wife that he had been cheating. She didn't divorce him, but her mourning of his death was severely complicated by his deathbed confession at the eleventh hour. That's just three of many examples. Now, when a divorce did ensue, these patients ended up very happily involved with someone else. But the take-home message is that disclosure needs to be undertaken

carefully, thoughtfully, purposefully, and with a good understanding and realistic expectation of what may come next.

Talking About Your Sexual Desires

Most experts agree that the best way to repair a relationship
after an affair is by talking openly and honestly about everything. That even means talking about your desires for other
lovers. Sometimes this conversation is best had with a trusted
friend or with a mental health professional. Occasionally, at
the appropriate time and place, you çan even have this conversation with your spouse.

Just as the secrecy of an affair *undermines* a loving relationship, sharing yourself openly and revealing your vulnerabilities actually *fosters love*. (Research has actually shown this to
be true. More about that in Chapter 11.) As Ken Adams, PhD,
an expert in compulsive sex and the author of *Silently Seduced:
When Parents Make Their Children Partners*, explained in a recent
talk that "a deeper experience of empathy and attachment is
the route to healing. I think it's the route to preventing infidelity, to stay deeply connected with your partner and vulnerable on a regular basis. That's hard work." He adds, "So many
couples are unprepared for what it really means to mate with
somebody long-term over the course of a lifetime, and having
the freedom to talk about the range of arousal and attraction,
and getting honest and vulnerable, can produce renewed excitement. We get preparation around everything *but* the fact
that we're going to be attracted to somebody else."

Another sex addiction expert, Dr. Alexandra Katehakis, author of *Erotic Intelligence*, agrees with Dr. Adams and Dr. Patrick

Carnes about how ill-prepared most people are for the work and communication required to sustain a long-term relationship. Dr. Katehakis attributes many relationship troubles with infidelity to a fundamental lack of effective communication about the changing nature of attraction. "If people get married when they're 22 or 25 and then they wake up and they're 45, they've been three or four different people in those decades." Difficulties come with the lack of "an active renegotiating conversation about who we are, what we like sexually, what we want sexually. . . . I think that's a big, big blind spot in our culture."

We'll talk lots more about these sexual wants, I promise. But first I want to spend some time on one of the most obvious yet surprisingly often overlooked elements of maintaining a strong, healthy, happy, constructive relationship: *emotional fidelity*.

Emotional Fidelity: A New Term for an Age-Old Reality

Go ahead and google it. If you search "emotional fidelity," the engine will come back at you with: "Did you mean: 'emotional infidelity'?" Nope, you didn't.

In my twenty-five years of psychiatry and couple's work, I've come to understand that *emotional fidelity* is the most overlooked aspect of relationship happiness. So far we've discussed the decisions that need to be made in the aftermath of infidelity and the basis for making those decisions. After the discovery of an affair, usually the focus is on sexual fidelity and blaming the partner who broke that vow. Yet the other component of infidelity, which I think looms larger and may actually be more destructive to relationships, is the challenge to the bonds of emotional fidelity.

Marriages often work best when both emotional fidelity and sexual fidelity are intact. So what exactly does that mean? Let's start with the easier one to understand: sexual fidelity. It means that you expect your partner will not have sexual relations with anyone else unless you agree to it. Even in most nonmonogamous relationships, in which couples grant each other explicit permission to have sex outside of their marriage (more on nonmonogamy in Chapter 12), many couples still expect that they will remain each other's primary sexual partner.

Emotional fidelity is a similar concept. I define it as committing to keep your partner as the central person in your life—your main source of connection and your primary confidant. Think back: when you met the person with whom you fell in love, you already had parents, maybe siblings, and likely close friends and other loved ones. When you fell in love, this former stranger suddenly became your best friend, your closest connection. You sometimes put your new lover's feelings even before your own. This stranger either took the place of your closest confidants or at least entered your inner circle of intimate relationships. As you fell in love, you talked every day. You started seeing each other every night. If something big happened in your life, the first person you wanted to tell was him/her. If something bothered you, theirs was the first shoulder you wanted to cry on. If something bad happened to you, you didn't blame it on this other person; instead, you saw them as a source of support and guidance. Some might call this codependency. Regardless, this emotional connection is generally what leads the couple to declare, "We are in love."

Please allow me to state this clearly: **You did not fall in love because you had sex. You fell in love because of emotional fidelity and your intention to continue it.**

Over the course of most long-term relationships, just as the sexual passion dies down, so too does this emotional connection. If you have children, your children (who are completely dependent on their parents) become more important (as well they should). A sick relative may also become more important as they need you more. Many people and activities can wind up taking the place of your spouse. A new job. Golf, basketball, or a card game. Aging parents. New and old friends who wind up getting way more attention and positive regard than your spouse. This connection to your spouse—the same person you once rushed to tell everything—fizzles. Instead of, "I can't wait to see you," when you walk in the door you might even think, "You again?"

This may be part and parcel of the extinguishing of the sexual flame, but I believe that the loss of emotional fidelity is the most destructive loss to the couple. The loss of emotional fidelity is essentially the failure to keep your promise of holding the other person in high regard and having their back at all times.

As I've stated, about half of people cheat simply because they can. They have no complaints with their marriage, and they report being happy with their spouses.

But many of those who are in the other half give reasons for cheating. I often hear, "My partner is just not that into sex anymore." When I ask my therapy group of male cheating patients what a spouse can do to prevent cheating, "Give them plenty of sex, and they'll never leave" is what they advise. Yet the *more* common reason that my patients, male and female alike, cite as why they cheat is because they don't feel that they can count on their partners. That special emotional connection they once shared has all but vanished.

The Challenges of Aging That Tear at Emotional Fidelity

"Too much water under the bridge" is how more than one person has explained the reasons for their estrangement from their spouse. Over the course of a long-term relationship there are many challenges to a couple's love. In time the marital union may become a less romantic connection and more akin to a business arrangement that functions solely to keep the family functioning.

As we know from previous chapters, novelty—new people and new situations—are extremely attractive to us. We are drawn to the new rat in the cage. We search for excitement in our lives—new relationships (even nonsexual ones), new careers, new pastimes, and new people who are more interesting than our *old* spouse.

Many married couples have a litany of good reasons why they don't feel emotionally connected: *who did what first, who did what more, who ignored whom, and who disrespected whom.* A long list. Psychoanalyst Eric Berne, MD, in his landmark book, *Games People Play*, described how many relationships fall apart because couples play unconscious games, holding onto grudges like some people collect stamps or baseball cards and blaming each other for the shortcomings and bad decisions in their own lives.

Aging itself can also wreak havoc on relationships. As men age they often engage less with others on a purely social level. They become more isolated and more dependent on their partner. Men often feel lonelier and worry that they matter less. They may experience and mourn the loss of their sexual appetite and abilities. They may feel less vital in the workforce.

Meanwhile middle-aged women face similar as well as different challenges. As they age women often report feeling sexually invisible to men in general and to their spouses in particular. In the workplace women face pressures similar to aging men. If they have been the primary caregiver for their children, they may face an identity crisis when their children leave home. These commonly occurring problems of aging lead many couples to blame each other for the biological, psychological, financial, and social realities of growing older. In the wake of these challenges it can be easy to find fault in our spouses and comfort in a new lover.

Watch What You Read

To help you keep a clear head about the value and viability of your long-term relationship, try not to get taken in by shallow advice or one-size-fits-all relationship "tips." Instead, trust your intuition. Popular media loves to provide quick fixes with insufficient regard for the complexities and varied nature of relationships. One study of popular articles about relationships featured in the top-five-selling men's magazines found that, in the author's opinion, bad advice was the norm. The researchers noted that "most advice was contrary to research on the formation of deep friendships and intimate relationships."

Psychiatrist Peter Kramer begins his book *Should You Leave?* with a quote from American novelist Peter De Vries that's worth repeating: "Why do people expect to be happily married when they are not individually happy? You go on so in America about marital contentment. Every magazine has an article with Nine Keys to it, or Seven Steps, as though the quest had any more sense to it or any more hope of fulfillment than the search for El Dorado." Dr. Kramer explains that a culture that prioritizes independence and autonomy over commitment may present obstacles to maintaining a long-term relationship. Such a culture can make us feel that we are entitled to that affair in order to reach some sexual ideal when the problem in the relationship may be with you and the solution may rest in compromise, realistic expectations, taking a good look at your own behaviors and thought patterns, and improving your communication skills.

Communication:
Breaking the Negative Infinity Loop

Speaking of communication skills, in the interest of reestablishing emotional fidelity I'd like to offer some guidance for breaking some old habits that are likely hurting your relationship.

The fundamental psychological force that describes the problems of long-term relationships is best diagrammed as an infinity loop, popularized by Dr. Sue Johnson and the book *Emotionally Focused Therapy for Couples,* which I first learned about from my colleague and cognitive-behavioral therapist Dr. Robert Filewich. The loop refers to how each person provokes the other, with couples ending up on an endless track of unmet requests and resentments, repeating the same arguments for decades.

When you first met your partner the loop was all positive. Good behavior reigned supreme in the beginning. Generosity was the code of conduct. Generally speaking, only nice and positive comments were exchanged, and any *un*pleasantries were suppressed. That approach issues forth the reciprocity of falling in love: you say one nice thing, they say something even nicer, and the positivity flows like a circuit.

In time a negative infinity loop often sprouts, even between the most well-intended couples. One person mistreats the other, the other mistreats them back, and suddenly resentments, anger, and impulsivity become king. You wind up like two angry siblings sitting in the backseat of your parents' car on a long trip, arguing over every little thing. All you can think about is how irritating this person is. How much harder they're making your life. How much you can hardly wait to get out of this car. Each person expresses anger—quietly fuming or loudly complaining—and the vortex of negativity builds. That is the negative infinity loop of relationships.

So in one paragraph I'm going to try to get you out of this negative infinity loop with some shock therapy. I apologize in advance for the profanity and graphic imagery that follows, but there's no better way for me to say it. My advice to my patients is: *STOP SHITTING ON YOUR PARTNER.* Yes, through our acts and our words, we defecate on our partner. We throw fits. We throw things against the wall. We blame them for what went wrong. We say or even yell nasty things that we would keep to ourselves in front of anyone else. We spew out hateful comments that blame them or condemn their personal failings. We put our partner in a box and assassinate their character. The words flow out of us like a long-awaited bowel movement. Like a toddler on the potty, it feels good to us, no matter how much of a mess we make. Yes, the bigger the better! I'm calling upon you to *stop pooping on your partner* because your partner and your partnership may never recover from the mess you make. I hope this vulgar image doesn't offend you but instead offers a metaphor that you never forget.

For example, one partner says, "All you want is sex." The other partner complains, "All you want is money." Because they see each other through shit-tinted glasses, where they once saw good intentions from their partner, now all they see is indifference, even malicious intent.

Being stuck in this negative feedback loop is the road to hell. And one way people seek escape is through an affair that takes us momentarily off the negativity track and gives us someone else to play with. But, as we've seen happen with some of the couples we've met in these pages, after the infatuation of newfound sex or romance wears off, a negative feedback loop with the new partner may very well develop as well—meanwhile the original relationship has died. There are definite steps couples can take to avoid this cycle of endless negativity. The first is having the awareness that regardless of who did what to whom, both partners need to commit to positive steps to sustain a long-term relationship. A second step is giving up your resentments and doing the good and proper things for your spouse and family.

Getting Emotional Fidelity Back

Even without the added burden of an affair, many spouses are loath to give up the resentments that eat away at the emotional connection between them. Emotional fidelity can be lost at any point in the relationship and at any age. To get it back, we need to work at being deserving of receiving emotional fidelity. Yes, you read that right: **we need to be deserving of receiving emotional fidelity**. Respect, acceptance, and forgiveness are important acts to restore emotional fidelity. If your partner has cheated on you, then respect, acceptance, and forgiveness may feel difficult, if not impossible. However, if your relationship has not gotten beyond the point of no return, you may want to consider how to restore the connection with the person to whom you once pledged your love.

Here's how:

- RESPECT: Find a way to rekindle respect for your partner. Dig deep in your soul. Take an inventory about how much your loss of respect for your partner has to do with them and how much has to do with you. How much have they failed you vs. how much did you idealize them early in the relationship only to devalue them later on? If your spouse needs to be better, teach them how, but try to give them the benefit of the doubt when it comes to respect.

- ACCEPTANCE: Be realistic. We've all heard the expression *perfection is the enemy of the good*. When you know someone over the course of many years, their imperfections can become glaring. Those of us who talk to couples for a living will tell you that it's rare for a person married for decades not to have some ambivalence about their long-term partner. Ambivalence is part and parcel of many healthy long-term relationships. The irrational search for a perfect mate or even a perfect constellation of sex-and-love partners is a ticket to unhappiness.

- FORGIVENESS: Be forgiving. When my patients complain about their wives or husbands, I like to joke, "I never meet the bad spouse!" In other words, we tend to focus on the problems and failures of our partner, while we often give ourselves a pass for our bad behaviors. Instead, I encourage you to pay more attention to your own role in causing problems and forgive your partner. If you can forgive your spouse, you may be able to make a lot of progress in your own life, even if you don't stay together.

Forgiveness is at the heart of what it means to love our fellow humans.

One strategy for counteracting the habits of holding grudges, second-guessing, or compiling a never-ending list of grievances is to take inventory with a "gratitude list." There's a saying used in twelve-step recovery programs that *gratitude is the best attitude.* It means that focusing on all the things you're grateful for can help you find happiness in life. This approach can also help you find happiness in your relationship.

As Dr. Patrick Carnes reminds us:

All relationships are challenges. The ultimate test of human life is making a successful long-term relationship. It is part of life's refining process that calls us into being better people. Family therapist Carl Whittaker once observed that all relationships are a struggle. It is simply a matter of finding the best "struggle" you can. Many times we find it is the one we are already in.

This question of *should I stay or should I go* boils down to: Can I love and be with my partner while expressing all aspects of myself, positive and negative, without fear? When most people reach the moment of dealing with an extramarital affair, they feel anything but safe and unconditionally accepted. Most feel ambivalent about their spouse. Both people in the relationship may question the love that once flowed freely between them. Both partners may feel psychologically unsafe. In other words, the decision of *should I stay or go* is hard to make in the midst of turmoil. This period of discovery and disclosure is a very tense time in your relationship and may be among the most challenging moments in your life. Several times I've urged you to *chill*—to stop and think before taking action. In the next chapter we'll talk about how to slowly work your way back into a sexual relationship with your spouse, if that's what you choose. As with my entire approach to the discovery of the affair, reengaging in sex should be thoughtful and part of a gentle reentry back into your relationship. There's nothing wrong with acting on unbridled passion with a spouse, but now is the time to take a more careful approach to repairing the damage and rebuilding a foundation for the long term.

chapter 11

Sexual healing and fidelity

A lthough emotional fidelity is paramount to sustaining long-term relationships, preserving a healthy sexual connection is also very important.

So When Do We Have Sex?

After discovering an affair, betrayed spouses sometimes swear off sex for the foreseeable future. Their anger and hurt lead them to repress all romantic desire. Some of these betrayed spouses develop what is called *sexual anorexia*, meaning their sexual self turns off. It may take them months—I've seen it take up to a year—to be willing to reengage in sex with their partner.

Or betrayed spouses may go in another direction. They may seek *revenge sex* with a new lover to get even, seek validation, and feel whole again. Sex becomes a weapon, under the control of negative emotions. I've had more than one couple go this route, with a betrayed wife going out and picking up strange men on the street, sometimes resulting in violent fights between her husband and her new male lover.

However, one of the more common responses I've come across in my practice is betrayed spouses seeking sex with their adulterous partners immediately, sometimes every day. Under the threat of separation, couples often find a renewed interest in each other. The idea of a third person in the mix turns some couples on, even as they struggle with betrayal, hurt, and shame. Although some spouses are repulsed when their partner has actually had sex with someone else, an outsider's desire for their spouse can be a turn-on. The fact that someone else finds you or your spouse attractive can get a couple's juices flowing. Suddenly, in the aftermath of transgression, a formerly ignored partner may now enjoy renewed interest from their once-disinterested spouse. Such is the human condition.

On top of that, couples often have makeup sex to reaffirm their lust and love, to lessen their fears of abandonment, to validate their hope that the relationship will last, and, sometimes, in a desperate attempt to keep the cheating spouse from straying again. What we lose in our rush to have sex, however, may be an opportunity to regain real intimacy.

I understand how it can feel like finding the missing link when a couple who has been together for years is suddenly struck with spontaneous and uncontrollable lust. However, with something as significant as the discovery of emotional or sexual affairs, I caution couples to think before jumping head-first back into sex.

The rush for immediate sexual gratification is often what led the couple to this infidelity in the first place. Plus, for many spouses, men and women alike, sexual engagement without feeling secure and safe in the relationship leaves them feeling much worse when the sex is over. (Recall how people feel when the brain's neurotransmitters of lust—dopamine and epinephrine—dissipate after orgasm, and the brain transmitters of bonding, oxytocin and vasopressin are released.) At that point your anger and disappointments are very likely to return.

Please trust me when I tell you that rushing into sex will not save your marriage. Don't get me wrong: sex is super important. It may be the best thing you've got going with your partner or may even be the only way you connect. But before jumping back in the sack, I urge you to first attend to your emotional needs. What do you want in order to feel safe? To feel loved? These are the kinds of questions you ought to ask yourself.

We often think of sex as a *need*, similar to our needs for air, food, and water. In actuality, sex is a drive—one that takes over our minds to make it feel like a need. A break from sex proves otherwise.

A Period of Reflection

After infidelity is discovered, I advise a period of abstinence— from a few days to no more than a few months—to create the opportunity for reflection and intention-setting, self- and relationship improvement, and the chance to live a healthier life with integrity. It is during the period of abstinence, however long or short, that the emotional healing discussed in the previous chapter occurs.

I've borrowed this idea from the sex addiction work of Dr. Patrick Carnes and his colleagues, who found it particularly useful for patients who engage in compulsive, dysfunctional sex. It is based on what alcoholic patients in recovery do when they start Alcoholics Anonymous—for the first ninety days they immerse themselves in daily twelve-step recovery meetings and dedicate themselves to deep and intense reflection. I've found it to be immensely helpful for *all* my patients struggling with infidelity, regardless of whether they're dealing with compulsions or addictions.

As we've discussed, the brain contains eighty-six billion neurons. Each neuron has connections to other neurons, which communicate with one another via synapses, making more possible connections between these neurons than the number of stars that exist in the known universe. The release of chemicals between the neurons creates and stores memories by changing—often strengthening—the synapses. The intensity and number of neurons that fire during an experience influence the connections that are forged. If an experience is linked to a powerful emotional drive—like an intense, forbidden affair—the chemical connections between the neurons forged is stronger, making the memory stronger as well. And if an experience occurs over and over—even if only in daydreams and fantasies—this further strengthens the memory. This repetition in your mind enhances the associations, linking this memory to many stimuli. Thus, the memory is strengthened as the synapses grow stronger still and more neurons are connected together, strengthening the memory further.

Just as repetitive thoughts and experiences empower memories, thwarting the repetition can weaken memories. One strategy I use in treating patients is to encourage a new, competing memory and repeat it in order to strengthen it over time. By helping patients think about their impulsive behaviors as a problem, a new belief—in the form of the thought, *this is a terrible idea*—begins to exist alongside the exciting memory, usurping some of the bandwidth once afforded to cravings for unhealthy sex.

In addition, I've learned through treating my patients who do have addictions that if you take something away, like a drug or bad behavior, you need to offer the promise of something good in return. That something could be a good relationship, a sense of doing the right thing, a clear conscience, great sex, or deep love. It needs to be something so good that someone can say at the end of the day, "This is better!"

If you think this approach to transforming one's longstanding sexual desires by replacing them with new thought and behavior patterns sounds easy, I'm sorry to disappoint you. Creating new neural pathways and behavioral patterns takes focused attention and determined hard work. It must be done with integrity and a clear sense of purpose.

For the person who has been unfaithful, a break from sex may be critically important. The affair has likely been an incredibly exciting, lustful pathway that's become etched into the neural system. It's not that the philanderer will forget their affair partner during a several-week sex break—in fact, absence may make their lust grow stronger—but this break will give the philanderer a chance to realize that their sex drive that led them to cheat does not actually control them and that they can survive without sex. The cooled-down brain, no longer immersed in hot longing for their affair partner, may, instead, refocus on their primary relationship and how to communicate with their partner.

There's an old Buddhist saying: "The mind takes its shape from whatever it rests upon." In this case the period of reflection helps the philanderer avoid resting their mind on the last extramarital sexual tryst or even the most recent time they masturbated and fantasized about the affair. During this period of reflection the mind rests on the more positive joys of integrity and love for their spouse and family.

More importantly, the break gives the couple a chance to contemplate how to proceed and may even allow them to fall in love again. I know it sounds corny, but there are many ways to communicate love and sensuality outside of genital contact. You and your partner can develop good communication. Touch each other, maybe even kiss, without going for the crotch. And honestly, in my experience, after the reboot the sex is likely to be better than ever.

Please consider taking a break from even thinking about sex. Even if you're horny as can be. No sex at all, not even masturbation and certainly no porn or materials like that. That's right: no masturbation! You will survive. You will not explode. And then, when you're ready for your partner, the sex is likely to be better than ever. Not too long a break—from a matter of weeks to three months, and that's all.

Take an Honest Look at Yourself and Your Desires

There is a joke that addicts in recovery tell one another: *How do you know if an addict is lying? His lips are moving.* Remember how I said that love and sex are the original addictions? That means we are all love and/or sex addicts in a way. As with any addiction, not only do we lie to our friends and family, but we lie to ourselves as well. That's called *denial*. Here is a simple yet revolutionary solution: instead of settling for lying and denial, how about striving for honesty and acceptance?

That is actually the whole goal of this book: to help us accept our human desires so we can be honest with ourselves and have honest dialogue with others so we don't wind up destroying our precious, deep love relationships with covert relationships. Honesty is a scary proposition. Often, usually with the best of intentions, we tell our partners what we think they want to hear. Honesty, however, requires telling people what they *don't* necessarily want to hear.

So what does rigorous honesty in sex look like? If you carelessly blurt out to your partner every desire you might have, particularly your frequent desires for another lover, you may end up unwittingly destroying your relationship and causing a betrayal trauma. So that's certainly not the approach I'm suggesting. Plus, we've all encountered people who say hurtful comments to us and then try to excuse it with "I was only being honest." Yet kind and respectful honest communication is the key to restoring love.

Honesty with your partner is important, but it is more important to be honest with yourself. That is the key task of his period of reflection. Ask yourself: What kind of life do you want? What kind of sacrifices are you willing to make? You know you can't have your cake and eat it too, so how are you going to make sure you don't destroy the good thing you have? This is the kind of honest dialogue you need to have *with yourself first.*

Even Anthony Survived the Reflection Period

Remember Anthony, the desire junkie, who would get so lost in fantasies or porn for hours at a time that his habit damaged his relationship with his wife and jeopardized his position at work? He found women intoxicating and always had them on his mind. He was ready for a change but didn't know how.

Anthony hated feeling so hooked. When he told his wife some of the details about his porn obsession, she was both angry and wanted nonstop sex with him to calm her fears about the fact that he found other women attractive. He and I talked about how sex with his wife wouldn't stop him from watching porn or even realizing his fantasies with women off screen.

We created a moratorium during which Anthony had to stop all sexual activity, including both porn and contact with his wife, for ninety days. The idea was to show him that his perceived need for sexual release was actually under his control. I also sent him to a twelve-step fellowship, Sex and Love Addicts Anonymous (SLAA), to hear how other men dealt with sexual obsessions. Having taken several patients to these meetings, I can tell you that there are *few* men who would *not* benefit from learning the lessons of SLAA. The principles of SLAA are based on Alcoholics Anonymous, using the same steps but applied to sex instead of alcohol. The program teaches men about the triggers that prompt them into dysfunctional sex, the value of integrity, the self-destructive elements of the way many men think about sex, and the lack of respect many men show toward their sex partners. Even if you're not an addict, going to SLAA is an eye-opening experience.

In the world of addiction there's another common saying: *those who fail to plan, plan to fail.* To give him the greatest chance for success, Anthony and I worked together to create a meticulous plan for avoiding triggers, which meant regulating his computer access. We talked about making him accountable to his wife so she could know what was happening with him. We spoke about exercise and self-care as well as techniques for how he could work through his anger and frustration without seeking fantasy to ease the pain. We discussed how his past as a peeping tom ogling women without their consent was actually an act of aggression whereby he sought power over women to help himself feel like more of a man. I gave this a professional label, *eroticized rage*, which is the use of sexual acts to prove oneself superior and powerful in order to make up for one's own sense of inferiority. Another troublesome trait Anthony and I spoke about was his sense of entitlement—the feeling of "I deserve this."

When Anthony's ninety days were over he had the best sex ever with his wife, over and over again. And although he still complained in our therapy group that his wife had less sexual desire than he did overall, Anthony knew he was a fortunate man. According to Anthony, his period of abstinence "taught me I can live without sex. It helped me learn how to control myself, to get a handle on my proclivities."

A year later he told me, "I feel like a new path has been cut into my brain. I do feel like I am capable of happiness and being a happy human being. Yes, I still have urges, and once in a while I slip"—meaning he looks at porn on rare occasion and very briefly—"I'm human. I'm not a robot. But I'll never stray from my wife. I feel my relationship with my wife gets stronger every day."

Both Partners Should Take a Break

Anthony's story might have convinced you of the benefits of the "problem" spouse taking a ninety-day break, but really my best advice is that both partners refrain from all sex and immerse themselves in a period of deep self-examination.

If you're the cheated-upon spouse, you probably feel this is not your problem—you should not have any work to do, nor should you suffer or be asked to sacrifice. You just want your cheating spouse fixed! I understand. In the case of Anthony, his wife was very unhappy about the sexual abstinence period. So we agreed that Anthony could provide her with sexual fulfillment, bringing her orgasm manually and orally, while he remained clothed.

You might ask: Doesn't that defeat the purpose of the abstinence? Wouldn't those acts arouse Anthony's sexuality? Not in Anthony's case. The goal of his sexual abstinence period was to avoid triggers for dysfunctional sexual behaviors. For Anthony that meant avoiding pornography, masturbation, and ejaculation, all of which he did to excess. Engaging in a loving and generous act with his wife was actually therapeutic for him. Furthermore, as a therapist I realize that I can't suggest something that will result in losing a spouse's cooperation—especially when the couple is working on trying to find their way back to one other. I didn't want to risk Anthony losing his wife's allegiance to her relationship or her support of Anthony's recovery, and I saw no harm in him servicing her. The possibility that this might tease him and help him refocus on his beautiful wife was a plus.

Each couple is unique, and each couple needs to find their own way toward reconciliation. Although in general I find it is best if both the cheater and the cheated-upon spouse engage in some degree of abstinence and reflection, giving everyone a chance to settle their sexual brains and figure out what's next, I also recognize that everyone has their own way of finding meaningful sex and love.

For those couples who love having sex, this reboot will only increase their desire. For those couples who haven't had sex in a while, it will give them a chance to contemplate their next steps and work on their relationship. Think of it like a prayer,

Lent, Ramadan, Yom Kippur, or a silent meditation. Every spiritual tradition has a period of abstinence, sacrifice, reflection, and contemplation built in. It is a period of time to think about how you have acted in the past and how you want to act in the future. Doesn't your primary relationship deserve such attention?

The First Sex Act: Talk

If the research is any indication, talking might actually be a great way to get ready for the restart of sex as well. As I mentioned briefly in Chapter 9, sharing vulnerabilities can be a powerful way for couples to reconnect after the upheaval caused by infidelity. In fact, intimacy alone has been shown to lead to arousal. Since the 1970s researchers have demonstrated that self-disclosure fosters attraction. In a 1990s study Arthur Aron, PhD, and his colleagues conducted a series of experiments to create emotional closeness in the lab by having two strangers ask each other increasingly personal, revealing questions and having them stare into each other's eyes. The researchers put strangers—heterosexual men and women, two at a time—together in a room for ninety minutes and instructed them to exchange increasingly intimate information. The researchers had developed thirty-six questions they thought would increase closeness and intimacy in strangers, like "What would constitute a perfect day for you?" and "Do you have a secret hunch on how you will die?" The researchers then had participants stare briefly into each other's eyes and directed them to say positive things toward one another. After that, they were free to never see each other again, but 30 percent of the subjects said the exercises made them feel closer to their conversation partner. In fact, the two first subjects in the experiment wound up marrying six months later!

In response to this research, relationship expert Dr. Patricia Love includes "exchanging intimate communications" as an element of her nine-step prescription for what she calls "hot monogamy." Other experts recommend the same. Because talking so openly is often a novel experience for them, explains Dr. Alexandra Katehakis, this new way of communicating can actually become a turn-on, even for couples who have been very close and intimate in past. "An intimate conversation and the novelty of that conversation creates heat between two people." What better warm-up for restarting sex?

In her book *Bad Match, Good Match: How to Tell the Difference*, Dr. Love advises that knowing where you and your partner fall on the desire spectrum is important. She says that many couples experience a desire discrepancy. People who have a high drive and feel compelled to explore sex with many partners are called *erotophilic*, meaning "lover of lust." Others who don't even feel desire until there is an emotional attachment are called *demisexual*. And because opposites often attract, marriage between a demisexual and an erotophilic is not uncommon, though it can be problematic. So what's a couple like this to do?

Dr. Love's first recommendation for the erotophillic is to understand what it's like for a demisexual to be vulnerable enough to have sex and then to see if that inspires any kind of compassion. If you happen to be the higher-desire partner, consider Dr. Love's recommendation to avoid being passive about your needs and instead ask for sex directly. Initiate sex. Become an expert in creating desire for your partner. Accept the fact that your partner may need more stimulation to become excited. And consider satisfying some of your purely physical needs on your own through masturbation.

For the partner with lower sexual desire, Dr. Love offers the following: "When you feel even the slightest pulse of desire, follow through on it. If you wait for a tidal wave of passion to wash over you, you may wait a long, long time." When I work with such patients, I suggest they read erotica or look at virtually anything that has a slight possibility of turning them on. Just talking about sex, feeling the liberation and freedom to say anything, can do a world of good.

One such patient was a forty-four-year-old woman who came to me having never experienced an orgasm through clitoral or vaginal contact. She had never felt comfortable being seen naked below the waist, and although she loved her husband dearly, she feared that only another man would be capable of bringing her an orgasm through a more typical route. Deeply pained by her lack of sexual response, she worried that maybe she was married to the wrong mate.

Through therapy I came to learn that she'd grown up in a family where any discussion of sex was forbidden. Her stern and disapproving father had shamed her about her body. Unfortunately, this sort of condemnation by fathers is quite common and sets up their daughters for a lifetime of shame. It became clear through our discussions that the problem was not her husband but her own sense of shame about her sexuality.

At first my patient didn't believe me. She thought the cause of her troubles must be that her husband wasn't passionate or compassionate enough. But as our work together progressed over the course of a year, she was slowly able to open up sexually through a combination of talking about sex and what turned her on as well as homework assignments involving solo masturbation; finally she allowed her husband to provide her with direct clitoral, vaginal, and vulvar stimulation. Lo and behold, she discovered that clitoral orgasms were actually easy to have with the man whom she loved so dearly. A decade later she's still married, monogamous, and very happy with her mate.

Are You Ready to Go at It? Your First Exercises

One benefit of the reflection period is that sometimes when you restart sex after a hiatus it can be quite spectacular. Other times it is a monumental undertaking. Although I want to offer you some guidelines for sex after the affair, the art of sex therapy is to create a roadmap collaboratively with an individual person or particular couple that is designed specifically for them and that respects their needs, traditions, and desires. Obviously that kind of customization is not possible here. But I'd like to offer some ideas for beginning exercises to use when you are ready for sex. Again: when you are ready for sex! Don't rush it! Now, this following part is pretty explicit, so I hope it doesn't offend.

Toward the end of the reflection period basic sex techniques, taken from the medical discipline of sex therapy, can help couples reach a more comfortable sexual space. The first, simple technique, developed by Masters and Johnson and popularized by Helen Singer Kaplan as a way to slowly regain a sensual connection without pressure, is called *sensate focus*. In the first step, Sensate Focus I, couples share a whole-body massage without genital contact. This means you caress each other but refrain from anything that could be considered sex. This touch reestablishes some trust and creates some excitement for the future without the pressure of sexual contact.

In the second step, Sensate Focus II, couples share a whole-body massage that includes pleasuring each other's genitals but without proceeding to any kind of intercourse. A third step, when *both* partners are ready, is allowing unrestricted sexual relations to occur, but you may want to wait until you feel 100 percent comfortable. As I'll discuss at the end of this chapter, the emphasis of sex, particularly when you restart, should be sharing and joy; rarely should the primary focus be on penetration, orgasm, performance, or outcome.

Critical to reestablishing trust after infidelity is recognizing that the feelings of each member of the couple need to be carefully considered and respected. Many betrayed partners will feel insecure about their bodies or their sexual selves. They may question their sexual abilities. They may feel ashamed. Some might even need to reclaim their own sexuality. When touched or even when just being naked, the betrayed partner may experience flashbacks. They may wonder, aloud or to themselves, *What was it like when you were with him/her? How did s/he respond? How did s/he look?* The whole experience can be daunting, so it is important to move slowly, purposefully, and lovingly.

What's Next? Get Educated

One benefit of restarting sex following a period of abstinence is having the chance to experience each other anew. The careful, step-by-step progression from touch to sex can offer the opportunity to move out of any sexual habits that feel more like a rut. The reflection period offers a "reset button" of sorts, so use it well!

Typically, once a couple settles on a way to make love, they rarely change and almost never discuss how they come together sexually in any meaningful way. There are a number of books and seminars that discuss improving your sex life, and many religious organizations sponsor sex and marriage education seminars as well. There is also plenty of information on the internet as well as legit sex shops where couples can learn about sex. For starters, I encourage couples to experiment with different sexual positions like having intercourse slowly to maximize every sensation, enjoying each millimeter of touch and insertion. Even if performing manual and oral sex or having intercourse feels intuitive, attentive foreplay can open whole new worlds of pleasure.

Be advised that the internet offers both a wealth of information and a cesspool of sex being subverted into negative energy. Be very thoughtful about what you watch or read. Seek out sites that are consistent with your values and traditions—religious and otherwise—and that provide sex-positive information. Avoid sites that offer typical misogynistic porn or are trying to sell you something stupid like a cream that will make your penis longer or websites that are a front for prostitution. Medical websites and nonprofit .org sites can offer reliable information.

Pleasuring a Woman

For starters, even if you think you're an expert, learn about your lover's anatomy. Although this book is not a sex primer, a couple of pointers are worthy of mention. The vulva (the exterior of the female genitals) can be a mystery for men and women alike, so much so that many people call this area the vagina (which is actually the vaginal canal). Many people don't appreciate that the seat of female arousal is the eight thousand nerve endings that reside on the clitoris. Nor do they realize that the clitoris disappears and retracts inside the lips of the vulva when a woman is on the verge of orgasm. The G-spot, inside the vaginal canal, is also poorly understood and controversial to this day, although many experts think that a nub of ultrasensitive tissue inside the vaginal canal (in the front and toward the middle of the vagina) contains nerves linked to the clitoris that sits on the outside.

The most important thing one can do is to talk to your lover. Ask what feels good. See if genital-breast, clitoral, vulvar, or vaginal stimulation is what they want. Sometimes both members of the couple are worried that the female genitalia are too dirty and/or confusing. They are afraid of talk about what they want, so they avoid any real discussion. Rooted in sexism and ignorance, these misunderstandings can be easily remedied by a few good books like *She Comes First* by Ian Kerner, PhD, and *The Art of Sexual Ecstasy* by Margo Anand. The Tantric and Orgasmic Meditation movements provide instruction on vaginal stimulation as well as practices for deeper emotional and physical connection among partners. In sum, communication and open-mindedness may dramatically improve your ability to pleasure a woman.

Pleasuring a Man

Popular discussion about pleasuring a man is sorely lacking. Yes, much of internet porn focuses on the penis, but porn usually perpetuates stereotypes. Yes, women's magazines routinely offer suggestions on how to satisfy your man, but the information provided is often inaccurate. A book called *He Comes Next: The Thinking Woman's Guide to Pleasuring a Man* by Ian Kerner, PhD, offers helpful information about male sexuality and could be a good resource to use instead. Surprisingly, many psychotherapists today still use a landmark book called *The New Male Sexuality* by Bernie Zilbergald, PhD, which was published back in 1978. In his book Zilbergald actually cautions men that they should not discuss their sexual problems with their females partners out of fear of turning them off and appearing weak. Yes, in the world today there is widespread discussion about taking Viagra and similar drugs. Yet most men who take Viagra don't tell their partners, and often their partners don't want to know.

Why are men and women so reluctant to have serious conversations about the challenges many men face when seeking enjoyable sexual function? "The last thing I can talk about is his flaccid cock," explained one of my female patients. "Talking about my problem makes it worse," said one of male patients. Our culture as a whole is wedded to the romance of strong men taking women who are mesmerized by their large, erect penises. Consequently, we struggle to talk about the reality of how to satisfy a man beyond acting like he's the conqueror, even though such a dynamic usually cannot be sustained and may ultimately doom a long-term sexual relationship.

Because the penis responds so easily, sometimes men's sexual partners think that all they need to do is locate his organ and it will snap to attention. However, some techniques are certain to please more than others. Techniques like kneading the penis with two hands (like you were kneading and rolling dough) and feathering it with a soft, sensual touch that barely touches the skin (like you were opening the plumes of a feather) may offer new options to try. Here the Tantric community also provides helpful instruction and information. There are many instructional videos online, and taking some time to learn and practice the art of sex is invaluable for any long-term relationship. I can't emphasize enough that for all genders, pleasure

One exercise to try

Even the most skilled lovers can benefit from a little experimentation. Here is one of umpteen ways to explore the varieties of sex play.

The game is called *Five Minutes of Surrender.* You get five minutes to do whatever you want to provide pleasure to your partner. Then you reverse roles, switching back and forth for six turns each during an hour of play. (Or play for less time, if you're in a rush. Just make sure you both get equal turns.) So what are the rules? Rule number one: pleasure only. The partner who is running their five-minutes of play must *only* do that which they believe to be exceedingly pleasurable to their partner. (Of course if your partner objects to what you're trying, shift gears.) As long as the partner who is in the passive position feels safe, their job is to relax, receive, enjoy, and surrender to pleasure. You can try out different positions, various oral or manual techniques, using inanimate objects, or playing with sexual fantasies. You can even touch your partner in an area that feels good but is not overtly sexual, just pleasing, like giving a five-minute neck or scalp massage. Rule number two? Obey the time limit before you switch roles so that the receiver becomes the doer and vice versa.

This game opens up the possibility of introducing a whole new set of sexual experiences. And best of all, it's mainly nonverbal. If you have *any question* about whether your partner will want what you are about to do, you must ask in advance. Of course the receiving partner can stop things at any time. Without pushing anything on anyone, this exercise avoids having lengthy discussions and negotiations; instead, each partner develops their sexual intuition, tries what they think they themselves might like and what they anticipate their partner will *love.* If your partner proposes something that feels terrible or objectionable, stop it. But if it's just unusual, you might consider giving it a five-minute chance.

can be found in many erogenous zones beyond the tip of the penis and clitoris. As you will learn, the mind is indeed the most erotic organ and the seat of pleasure. For your partner, being an open, explorative, communicative, well-intentioned, and artistic lover is worth your weight in gold.

Sometimes Medication Can Help

When it comes to sexual issues in a relationship, the best solution is a candid conversation about sexual pleasure with your partner. However, I would be remiss if I didn't mention that there are also a very few situations in which medications may be helpful. Certainly before you even consider taking a medication for any reason, let alone a sexual one, you need a full exam with blood tests assessing thyroid and other bodily functions, plus a darn good medical reason for taking a pill. Here are a few decent motivations.

Sometimes sex with a long-term partner is a challenge because you just don't get that excited. No question about it, this is a psychological problem that you need to talk through. But meds can help too. In all likelihood, during an affair a female philanderer got incredibly lubricated and the male philanderer got rock-hard erections. Now that you're with your long-term partner, you may not only miss that rush of having a "new rat in your cage" but also feel nervous about sex. These feelings can also inhibit lubrication and erection. In these cases a drug like Viagra can be useful.

Viagra only improves the plumbing, however. The medication only works *after* you get turned on—either through touch or by just having sexy thoughts. Viagra increases genital blood engorgement and keeps blood in the genitals. Although

Viagra doesn't act directly on the brain and does not increase the brain's sexual desire per se, the drug may enhance the feedback loop between the brain and genitals. In other words, if a person feels more arousal because their genitals are engorged and experiences more of a genital response to touch and thought, these may combine to create more desire.

Viagra, Cialis, and Levitra are only FDA approved for men. Although I, among other doctors, have published case studies on using Viagra for women, the results are mixed. In sum, although Viagra can help women slightly, it is not yet approved for that purpose, and organic oils such as coconut oil or, when properly prescribed, estrogen creams may be safer options to increase lubrication.

If the problem is that one partner has a generally low desire for sex, other meds may be helpful. Medications that increase the brain's neurotransmitter of desire, dopamine, like Wellbutrin, Filbanserin, and Buspar, may increase sexual desire. A specialist may even prescribe hormonal treatments in pill form like testosterone to increase desire and arousal in both men and women if naturally occurring testosterone levels are documented to be low on blood tests and when there are no risk factors, such as cancer, that contraindicate hormonal treatments.

If the problem is the reverse, meaning a person is oversexed or even addicted to sex, resulting in the intense desire to cheat, other medications can help. This is a last resort, but there are many medicines that can be taken for this kind of problem. People with sexual compulsivity who need their sexual desires decreased can take Prozac, Zoloft, or Lexapro, to name a few. At the same time, these meds also reduce anxiety and depression. The choice of which medications are prescribed for sexual impulsivity is based on the other co-occurring symptoms associated with the acting out. For instance, people who also have signs of bipolar disorder, which is associated with impulsive sexual acting out, may benefit from mood stabilizers such as lithium, Depakote, and Lamictal. Likewise, these drugs help modulate impulsivity in people who are risk takers and thrill seekers, helping people avoid destructive sexual encounters.

Many people commit infidelity out of boredom. A small fraction of these bored people have attention deficit disorders (ADD), which we've discussed earlier as a problem of needing super-intense stimulation to feel engaged. For them, nonaddictive ADD medications may change their lives for the better and may even lead them to be less sexually impulsive.

There have been medical reports about certain aphrodisiac herbs and natural vitamins that promote sexual desire, but unfortunately we lack significant scientific data to support their use. Recreational drugs can also promote sexual desire. Many people drink alcohol to become disinhibited and engage more freely in sex. For people without substance abuse problems, sometimes a drink may be helpful, no doubt. However, amphetamine-based or hallucinogenic drugs used to promote sexual behaviors, such as molly, crystal meth, and ecstasy, are not only illegal but can also be extremely dangerous to consume.

Even if you opt for a medicinal boost to your sex life, please remember that sex begins and ends in your mind. Therefore, by working on your thoughts, emotional intimacy, and talking to your partner, you stand the best chance of making your sex life sexier.

Great Sex After Infidelity Is Nearly Always Possible

There are very few couples in my practice who, after they talk and try to work things out, don't have a great sex life. Once they bypass the psychological hurdles, they find it relatively easy to get back in a great sexual groove. But what about if your biological sex drive is diminished? When you are tired of the same old partner? And how about if, on top of that, you discover that your spouse's infidelity involved something completely out of your personal comfort zone, like sex with a same-gender person? That was the situation faced by Jack and Nellie, both in their late fifties, who had been married for more than three decades.

As with many older couples, Jack and Nellie had age-related changes. Jack had decreased penile sensitivity and difficulty maintaining an erection. Nellie had decreased vaginal elasticity and moisture. Jack had been a wonderful and dedicated husband for decades, yet he secretly longed for something he felt Nellie could not provide. Jack always felt turned on by men and was captivated by the idea of receiving anal sex. Jack was married to a woman and was happy with his wife. Yet as he hit his midlife crisis and feared dying without satisfying his lusts, Jack felt his sexual yearnings more strongly.

While the couple was on vacation at a spa resort, Jack tried to have sex with a willing male massage therapist. They got as far as the massage therapist giving Jack oral sex, but Jack abruptly ended the session. Perhaps it was paranoia or guilt, but he feared getting hurt by the massage therapist's boss if the staff found out. Jack immediately confessed to Nellie, and the couple quickly left the resort.

This might have ended many other relationships or at least caused irreparable damage. Not for this couple, though. Jack was fortunate to have a wife willing to talk through their issues. He entered therapy. Nellie was truly supportive of Jack and didn't just want him "fixed" by his therapist—she wanted both of them to be happy.

They spoke candidly. Now that their hormones were in decline, they both agreed to add some extra oomph to their sex life. A nonmonogamous relationship was not acceptable to Nellie nor was it something Jack actually wanted. Instead, they discussed finding new ways to make love. Through their open conversations they came up with a plan. When next they had sex, Nellie used a vibrator nestled between the lips of her vulva to help bring herself to the orgasms that were becoming more elusive with age. Jack masturbated himself to completion as Nellie inserted a dildo—in this case, a penis-sized latex phallus—into his anus. They timed it so they orgasmed at nearly the same time. Although their approach might turn off some couples, it works for Jack and Nellie. Jack feels more in love with his wife than ever for her willingness to experiment and give him what he desired. In fact, they both feel they're incredibly lucky to have each other, enjoying a new phase in their sex life as a couple. They feel no shame, no judgment—just gratitude.

Reframing Our Notions About Sex

Infidelity starts long before the first illicit kiss. It starts with our distorted thinking and unrealistic expectations. Here are a few relationship principles to explore for maximizing romantic and hedonistic pleasure with your long-term partner.

Honest and Well-Intended Communication (Without the Goal of Manipulation)
This first principle has to do less with specific sex acts and more with how partners approach each other. Talking about sex in a way that communicates your intimate feelings (without

judgment, criticism, or comparisons to former lovers or others) can bring a deeper bond between you and your partner and create the openness and trust that helps you have better sex. Sure, we enjoy thrills. Forbidden sex is hot. But if we truly feel threatened and scared and our bodies go into *fight-or-flight mode,* our genitals simply do not work in a sexual manner. So feeling safe, loved, and confident that you can trust your partner and share intimate thoughts and feelings creates the right atmosphere.

Egoless Sex and Love
(Without the Goal of Self-Importance)

Men and women often fall in love and have sex to feel good about themselves. Yet ego-driven love and sex are ultimately just a temporary fix for a fragile ego. One of the major themes of this book concerns how our egos get us in trouble. Our need for validation from a new person can lead us toward infidelity. If there's one place where we should put our ego to rest, however, it's in the bedroom. When you are with your lover, you have nothing to prove; instead, focus on the sensations of pleasure and experience a loving connection.

Anorgasmic Sex (Without the Goal of Orgasm)

Focusing on the orgasm can interfere with attachment. Unless you are trying to have a baby, in which case male ejaculation is ultimately a priority, I encourage you to focus on the richness of sexual experience. Orgasms last only a few seconds, but good sex can last for hours and can sustain a relationship for a lifetime. Try to keep the focus on attachment, which is really why you've ended up in the bedroom anyway. Orgasms are great, but they can interfere with the goal of making and confirming your love.

Dispassionate Sex and Love
(Without the Goal of Passion)

Intense passion may have happened during the forbidden sex of the affair and at the beginning of your marriage. It can happen again, and experiencing that mad lust and urgency can be nice, but it can't be replicated every time you have sex throughout a long-term relationship. The pressure to feel unbridled *passion* (rather than letting it rise naturally) is more theater than reality. It makes us need new lovers and new audiences to watch our act. The alternative that I'm recommending is: "forget the act." Allow sex to be dispassionate: open, curious, losing track of time and space, communicative, and disconnected from urgency.

Dispassion, a concept based on Buddhist, Hindu, and Tantric philosophies, is difficult to explain. In Western thought dispassion is considered something bad. It implies a lack of commitment or enthusiasm, sometimes signifying an overly rational mind devoid of emotion or a person who is operating in a dutiful way. In our Western way of thinking, cold dispassion seems to be the opposite of hot sex.

In Eastern thought, however, dispassion lies at the heart of the spiritual philosophy. It is the antidote for frenetic worry. It means to not take everything so seriously because your worries are sometimes mistaken and the intense meanings that you attach to a situation (which may make you nutty) are often wrong. Dispassion means we adopt a more "Zen-like" or an "enlightened" approach. It means that you approach life's challenges with the perspective of a wise elder who has seen it all and, through their vast experiences, realizes that what often gets us all worked up is a waste of our time.

So how do you attain this dispassion, also known as *equanimity,* in sex? It means you approach sex not as a win/lose situation or a proving ground for your relationship; instead, you let whatever happens happen, without judgment or anxiety. When you get in bed with your partner, you dedicate yourself to their pleasure and yours, and you focus on your shared love. You try not to let other thoughts interfere with your mission.

If you are the betrayed partner, you don't focus on *Am I as good as the affair partner?* If you're the cheating spouse, you don't get worked up by *What does it mean that I'm thinking about my affair partner while I'm having sex with my spouse?* You let these thoughts pass through your mind like water flows through a sieve. Dispassion means that you are accepting of and patient with yourself and your partner, that you proceed with the attitude that *no matter the outcome, it will all be okay.* You don't sit in judgment but rather proceed with the intention of making love and creating pleasure.

chapter 12

Sex and love with more than one: Do open relationships work?

Although many of us believe that there can be few experiences as rewarding as having one dedicated, romantic partner throughout our lifetime, nonmonogamous
alternatives have helped many couples achieve unexpected
balance in their relationships. As I said in the Introduction,
this book is not a diatribe for monogamy but rather an argument for integrity, passion, and compassion. In that spirit, let's
talk about how some couples are exploring nonmonogamous
relationships and what we can all learn from their experiences.

Couples have long sought to resolve the challenges of
heated passion fading over time as well as what scientists call

humans' "dual reproductive strategies" to both pair up long term and to mate with many people. One way to do this is to open the door of their relationship to others—establishing ethical nonmonogamous parameters. In these arrangements—perhaps even more so than in traditional marriages—honesty is crucial.

Nonmonogamous Arrangements

Although there are, of course, as many relationship configurations as there are individual couples, nonmonogamous arrangements can be divided into two general categories. One option is to have recreational sex partners other than your mate, while your spouse remains your lifelong, primary partner. You remain emotionally, socially, and economically committed to each other—sometimes sexually engaged with each other and sometimes not—as you also pursue other sex partners.

Another option is *polyamory* (which means "many loves"), in which you may have several mates with whom you share deep emotional and sexual bonds, without an exclusive attachment promised to any one person—although you may promise an exclusive commitment to a closed set of certain individuals that's agreed upon by all parties. The social, emotional, economic, and cohabitation commitments of such relationships can take many forms. Polyamory can allow for a variety of family configurations, with or without children, and can offer many of the financial, emotional, and social perks of other long-term relationships.

So these are perfect, easy solutions for wanting to have sex and love outside your relationship without infidelity, right?

Unicorns are real

Penelope was a twenty-seven-year-old, successful junior executive who was unclear about her sexual orientation. She knew she preferred men for emotional relationships and women for casual sexual encounters. She had a devoted boyfriend, but she left him to explore a man she was crushing on because she didn't want to cheat. But before long, that exploration ended. Now uncommitted, Penelope, who'd been desiring sex with women, was intrigued by the idea of a threesome with a couple in an open, nonmonogamous relationship. On a website dedicated to finding such connections, Penelope found a married couple her age. Two thirty-year-olds who'd been married for seven years, Eddy and Samantha, had decided to spice up their sex life with a third partner. They placed an ad looking for what is called a *unicorn* (a woman who is purportedly a rare find) who would want to join the couple for sex only. Penelope says, "For them it was a way to keep things exciting and do different things together, sexually." For Penelope it became a chance to explore her sexuality safely and respectfully in an out-of-the-box way.

When the three first met at a bar, Penelope had a costume in her bag: midthigh, spandex American flag shorts. "We ended up

Not at all! All relationships require negotiation and hard work, including nonmonogamous ones. Cheating is still an issue in these relationships as well, whenever someone breaks the rules that both/all relationship partners have agreed to.

In the recreational sex option, maybe you're okay with your partner having sex with two other people, but they want sex with four. Or maybe the rules you establish together allow for sex with others but prohibit love. Good luck with that!

back in my place, tried on costumes, and hooked up." Nearly every month for a year now, they've all gotten together to have sex. "I really like being a third," Penelope explains. "I like both people." Through her good fortune (and due diligence) she found a couple in which both partners were excited about the idea of a threesome and who had support from their friends that helped them establish a nontraditional relationship without any lying, cheating, or coercion. Penelope says their three-ways have helped the couple's relationship. They periodically send Penelope Snapchat photos and videos of the two of them having sex, which "makes it more exciting for them."

If existing trends continue, nonmonogamy may become more mainstream. In addition to her unicorn role, Penelope hopes to find a partner interested in a committed relationship that includes nonmonogamy. She knows from her friends, whose relationships have the chemistry and integrity to maintain honest nonmonogamous relationships, that such an arrangement is possible. "Because everyone knows the statistics now [about how commonly cheating occurs], it makes it so that people are more open-minded about ways to prevent that from happening," she says.

Or, in the polyamory situation, perhaps you and your partner(s) decide that loving someone else is okay as long as it's not a certain kind of partner who may be disruptive to the family unit. Yet, as we all know, we often wind up wanting what we cannot have. Rule breaking is a problem in monogamous and nonmonogamous relationships alike because when we're dealing with infidelity, we're dealing with the all-too-human tendencies to cheat, lie, misbehave, be intensely driven by our desires, and simply want something different and new.

Finding Love in a Sea of Choices

In her 2017 *New York Times* Modern Love column, "I Had 1,946 Suitors. Too Bad I Only Wanted One," Lauren Peterson offered a contrasting perspective on what she saw as a trend away from monogamy. Her experience with online dating–through the app Bumble, which calls shopping for a mate a "game"– had left her bobbing about in a sea of available men, none of whom wanted monogamy. "I wanted to leave the game behind and develop something special, if only for a short time," Lauren lamented. After she entered her profile and the characteristics she desired in a mate, Lauren landed 1,946 matches. With so many choices available at the swipe of a thumb, this app likely stimulates its users' brain's reward centers, instilling in them the hope that the next swipe will be better than the last. But what is "best" anyway?

Lauren recounted the tale of one guy she met whom she liked a lot. They slept together on Monday nights for six weeks. After the sixth week of sex sleepovers, she sheepishly wanted to text something personal and finally sent three words: "I like you."

"I like you too," he replied. Yet her proclamation moved the couple toward their inevitable ending. He had a "thing" about monogamy, he told her.

"Monogamy requires more sacrifice than ever," Lauren explained in her piece. Today's daters have to say no to a plethora of possibilities. Even if someone actually *is* looking for a long-term relationship and is willing to commit to monogamy with the right person, there's a ready temptation to play the field, enjoying recreational sex while continuing to shop around. Of course, when partners come together and have sex with differing objectives, it can lead to some very bad blood.

The Recreational Sex Interlude

Lest you think Millennials are the only ones dabbling with nonmonogamous solutions, allow me to tell you about Clara and Lenny, who had married in their twenties and were now in their fifties. "The idea that we would spend the rest of our lives without the pleasure of kissing another person, for both of us, it felt like something was missing," Lenny explains. Clara agreed. The notion of never being with another person struck them both as "sad and constricting."

It wasn't just that they wanted variety; they wanted spice and heat and affirmation, and what they discovered was the chance to see themselves and each other differently. Before they decided to open up their marriage, the two had been arguing. Clara had gained weight, and Lenny criticized her for it. Clara felt unappreciated and took to drinking to escape her unhappiness. Their sex life was dull. As we've seen in the couples we've met previously, this set the stage for straying.

Through Facebook Clara reconnected with an old friend she'd known before she married. When their exchanges became flirtatious, Clara told Lenny that she would like to speak to him on the phone and then possibly even meet. She had no intention of sneaking behind Lenny's back. They had always had an honest and direct relationship. Even though they were both angry, their love and respect for each other was never in question. Neither hinted at divorce. Neither had any interest in destroying the good in their lives, with their two children and a home that they had built themselves. Both just wanted happiness.

According to Clara, Lenny's immediate response was disheartened, "I would prefer you not have sex with him." To which Clara, uncertain of the outcome of her meeting, honestly responded, "I can't promise that." But she added that she would not have any contact whatsoever with him if Lenny really objected. Lenny asked, "Can I do the same thing?" She assured him, "Of course." After all, it was the least she could offer. Lenny explained his thought process at the time this way: *Being able to have sex with someone other than my wife. Are you kidding? It felt like I'd won the lottery!* Lenny immediately looked up an old girlfriend.

Lenny and Clara arranged to meet their prospective lovers on the same weekend so that neither of them would be left alone and upset. Lenny recalls the first of several encounters with his reunited lover, in which they started groping each other in the cab from the airport where they met: "When we got together, we just had sex all weekend long. That's what the weekends were all about!"

For Clara it was the emotional connection that she craved, and the sex came after. "I just loved the attention I was getting from this person who seemed to just think I walked on water and who fell in love with me, and I fell in love back." Clara's relationship with her paramour "grew out of an emotional itch of feeling underappreciated at home and not having a lot of closeness to my husband at the time and having someone else come along who would provide those things in spades. And then it became sexual because we fell in love. . . . It totally reactivated my sex drive, which had been in the basement for a while." Lenny's lover, meanwhile, was someone with whom he saw no long-term romance potential, despite how well she met his "unmet needs."

Clara and Lenny's extramarital escapades went on for a year. And through their consensual nonmonogamy they not only became closer but also began having hot sex with each other again. The long-married couple became more affectionate. Although Lenny didn't want to know about Clara's other relationship, she was curious about his. Lenny found the fact that they could talk about it reassuring.

Both partners thought the experience helped the marriage. For Clara, the appreciation she got from her boyfriend helped her feel better about herself and her life. She felt attractive again, and that helped bring back her sex drive. "At the same time, because my husband was happy having sex with someone else, he became much more appreciative, and much less critical." That, she said, improved their entire relationship, which wound up improving their sex life.

The success of opening up their marriage, Clara is quick to point out, was predicated on the fact that there was no cheating involved. "This was not infidelity. I did not want to be unfaithful. I had to get permission before I would do anything like this," she explains. "We had rules. We were very thoughtful." The two agreed not to talk to their outside partners in mixed company and did their best to plan rendezvous for when neither would be sitting at home wondering what was happening with the other.

For Lenny, eventually the novelty wore off. Immediately after the sex with his new lover was over, he wanted to leave. He found himself wondering, *What am I doing with this woman?* When Clara's lover wanted to marry her, she responded to his clinginess by ending it. Each of them tried relationships with other people but soon discovered that other lovers were more trouble than they were worth. At the same time, their marriage was renewed. They appreciated each other more. Their sex life together increased in lust and frequency. And they both felt incredibly grateful to the other for being willing to try a new arrangement.

"Not many people would be able to handle this," said Clara. "A lot of people would feel very, very threatened, but we didn't." Clara and Lenny had honestly acknowledged their curiosity about exploring other people, but both made it clear from the get-go that their relationship was the one that mattered most. "I don't need to do that again," Clara says. "We've seen that movie. Now we both feel so much gratitude for allowing each other to scratch that itch and be okay with it."

Five years later their marriage is reaping the benefits of their willingness to experiment and problem solve as well as all they've learned about themselves and each other. They have grown, both together and as individuals, instead of stagnating as a couple. If you ask me, the key to their success was that they never lost emotional fidelity. They never made each other second fiddle. Their approach to the problems of their marriage, although unusual and not something I could recommend for most people, was very considerate and collaborative. They took pains to avoid hurting each other or rub their extramarital relationships in each other's faces. Every step of the way their choices embodied the idea that emotional fidelity is critical.

All in the Family

Fory-three-year-old Cheri tried monogamy, but after her "normal marriage" ended, she knew she needed more stimulation than monogamy could provide. With her first match on eharmony.com, she and her prospective date agreed on the telephone to be polyamorous. Twelve years later she and her match have a "super-happy," "healthy," poly marriage. Cheri should know, because in the process she earned a doctorate in sexology and developed a career as a polyamory expert.

A few years into her second marriage she met Mark, the man who became her additional life partner. Cheri and her husband had agreed before she and Mark had gotten romantically involved that the two could date. Seven years later both couples are still together. Up until last year the three of them lived in one house along with Cheri's sixteen-year-old son from her previous marriage. The men are best friends and as close as brothers. A year ago Mark built a home, and now Cheri maintains a separate home with him and splits her time between living with each of her two guys.

What Does the Research Say?

Clara and Lenny's success stemmed from their overarching desire to stay together. Even as they wanted to spice things up, they were exponentially more dedicated to not blowing their lives apart. They also were both quick to realize that the faults in their lives were due less to their partners and more to something "internal," as they put it, meaning it was something within themselves that required self-reflection and taking responsibility for their own shortcomings.

Cheri didn't think there was anything internal to fix, nor did Penelope. These two women, nearly a generation apart, decided that they were okay just as they were. Instead, the constructs of their sex/romantic lives needed to change. They needed to leave the monogamous paradigm and live and love in a nonmonogamous world. A few decades earlier Penelope and Cheri would have been considered freaks, probably diagnosed by psychiatrists as nymphomaniacs. Today they are part of an emerging and viable movement called *nonmonogamy*.

A growing popular literature on the advantages of sexual encounters outside a primary relationship suggests that they can lead to self-growth and self-actualization. Authors like Esther Perel and Dan Savage have written about the personal growth that can come from *extradyadic sex* (a research term for sex outside the *dyad*, or a committed couple). A 1997 guide to polyamory, *The Ethical Slut: A Guide to Infinite Sexual Possibilities* by Dossie Easton and Janet W. Hardy, introduced mainstream audiences to the rules of ethically maintaining multiple relationships.

More than one patient has reported to me that, in the midst of a marital crisis, they read *The Ethical Slut* cover to cover and drew up a careful and thoughtful list of dos and don'ts. Falling in love or just seeing a sexual partner repeatedly is usually on the list of don'ts. But, as they say, no plan survives contact with the enemy. Although couples often set out to explore other people according to the rules they've established, once a person finds someone more enticing and alluring than their partner, the rulebook goes out the window. Even with the best of intentions, it can be hard to follow the rules in matters of the heart—especially given the fact that sexual attraction itself often gets fired up by notions of rule breaking and desiring what's forbidden.

What Does Animal Research Tell Us About Monogamy?

According to animal researcher Larry Young, PhD, "Our brains, from a biological perspective, are not designed to make us want to be faithful." We are the product of biology, which selects for a mating system focused on transmitting genes to the next generation. If a female sees a male who is healthier and has better genes than her partner, it is to her advantage to mate with him for greater diversity in the offspring. Similarly, if a male mates with another female, he increases his likelihood of having more offspring and more survival of his progeny. That, among animals, is the most adaptive strategy. Dr. Young says that in order to be monogamous as a member of the animal kingdom, "You're going against some hard-wiring to make that happen."

Only 3 percent of male and female mammals (which includes a wide-ranging array of animals, from mice to humans) stay together after mating to raise offspring (which scientists call *social monogamy*). When it comes to the group of mammals called primates—those mammals with the largest, most complex, and specialized brains—an estimated 15 percent of primates stay together to rear their young.

Monogamous Voles, Revisited

Remember the highly researched prairie voles? As you'll recall from Chapter 3, it seemed at first that the prairie voles mated for life and were held up as paragons of monogamous virtue, a long sought "holy grail" example of fidelity in mammals that many hoped could be studied to help humans. Setting aside the fact that this whole line of thinking disregarded the reality that voles are not humans but rather rodents who live in dirt, the voles' lifelong bonds, scientists thought, provided evidence against the prevailing wisdom that we humans had evolved to be philandering. When researchers did paternity tests, however, the storyline fell apart.

The researchers found that the prairie pups sometimes had a different father than the vole dads who were raising them. In other words, the prairie vole females *do* mate outside their primary relationship, although not as much as the meadow voles. Evidently, although the prairie voles may have had good bonding skills and formed a lasting family unit, they also sometimes succumbed to animal lust. This led vole researchers to distinguish between *social monogamy* and *sexual monogamy*. The prairie voles were socially monogamous, joining their lives together, but not always sexual monogamous, meaning mating exclusively with one partner forever.

The extra-relationship mating of female prairie voles that Dr. Susan Carter, executive director of the Kinsey Institute, observed in her laboratory studies did not disrupt the vole family—it was for sex only. After the female prairie vole mated with another male, Carter wrote in the journal *Nature*, "she attacked him, ran him off and went back to her established partner."

Although most prairie voles will not spend time with a newly introduced vole, 20 percent of "monogamous" voles will have sex with the new vole, but they always return to their primary partner. That still makes the prairie voles relatively faithful, as 80 percent of them remain sexually exclusive.

We humans have a peculiar use of the word *monogamy*. We have come to think of monogamy as being completely faithful, romantically and sexually, to one partner. Biologists, however, make a distinction between social monogamy (or pair bonding to rear young together) and sexual monogamy (which is sexual exclusivity with a single partner.) Still, much of the scientific research and many books on monogamy have failed to understand this distinction.

One of the breakthroughs in the vole research occurred when one curious researcher took an interest in the voles that didn't fit the mold. When individual prairie voles strayed, mating with a vole not their partner, some labs got rid of the gallivanting animals, seeing them as somehow defective. But Mohamed Kabbaj, PhD, professor of biomedical science and neuroscience at Florida State University who has worked with voles for six years, studied these uncommon animals even more closely. He told me what he'd observed: that one out of ten male prairie voles mated outside of their partnership. What distinguished the cheats from the faithful? The voles that strayed had higher testosterone levels. As it turns out, the same is true for humans: both men and women who commit more infidelity tend to have higher levels of testosterone.

According to Cornell University vole researcher Dr. Alex Ophir, who studies voles not in the lab but in their natural habitat, the percent of cheating voles is actually over 20 percent. He says that the so-called monogamous prairie voles may be a better model for love and attachment than we care to admit—they stay together, but 20 to 25 percent stray, then return to their mates. Interestingly, this is roughly the same percentage of monogamous humans who stray. The real difference between the monogamous voles and monogamous people is that among the animals female voles stray more often than male voles.

Even among animals that do seem to make exclusive life-long bonds, it's possible to get them to stray by altering their brain chemistry. The more we study animals, the more we find that although they may remain connected one partner for a mating season (in the case of birds) or a lifetime (in the case of the voles), when it comes to sexual fidelity, they may be more *monogamish* than monogamous.

Humans, Naturally Monogamous or Not?

Unlike most mammals, humans are biologically hard-wired to fall in love and stay together as a couple to raise our children, but we also have our ancestors' philandering genes. Genetically speaking, the most highly successful humans had the most partners and parented the most children. In the past, success was measured by conquest. The conqueror Genghis Khan, as one colorful example, was said to have sired hundreds of children and, as a result, his tribe is said to have left his genetic imprint on 0.5 percent of the world's male population today.

Dr. Helen Fisher, the biological anthropologist who told us in Chapter 3 about humans' dual—and conflicting—reproductive strategies to both bond and stray, told me that throughout her forty years of studying love, sex, and the brain in more than forty cultures, "the single-most interesting thing I've ever read was a study by Shirley Glass in 1985 that found that 56 percent of adulterous men and 34 percent of adulterous women reported being in happy or very happy marriages."

In a similar vein, a 2014 survey on a UK dating site called Elite Singles asked 667 men and women about why they had strayed from their partners. Most men (55 percent) could not identify a reason for being unfaithful. Dr. Fisher's answer to why? "Because of basic Darwinian mechanisms to pass on your DNA. Many people are not adulterous because they are in unhappy relationships or because of bad childhoods. They are just adulterous because they are!" This finding offers us yet another reminder that, as devastating as they can be for a relationship, affairs are very often "not personal."

Increasingly, there is an emerging movement of people who view nonmonogamy as a solution. However, they soon realize that navigating several relationships is no cakewalk, as nonmonogamy often requires exponentially more arranging, agreements, scheduling, honesty, and self-discipline than monogamy because more people are involved.

Sure, experts can cite primitive tribes in remote places and moments in world history in which nonmonogamy was an accepted practice. Even today some communities in European and Asian countries have much more relaxed attitudes when it comes to sex with someone other than one's spouse. But the great majority of Americans still value, want, and expect monogamy. Studies indicate that 75.8 percent of Americans endorsed the idea that sex with someone other than their spouse is "always wrong," whereas only 2.3 percent said it is "not wrong at all." Is our expectation of monogamy still relevant, and does it have merit for the remainder of the twenty-first century?

Well, what do the social scientists say? An emerging group of social scientists and medical experts advance and advocate for nonmonogamous arrangements, but they are in the minority. Most psychologists and family therapists take a live-and-let-live attitude that permits consenting couples to make personal decisions about monogamy and nonmonogamy. Although they theoretically support nonmonogamy, the vast majority of licensed mental health professionals counsel couples within a promonogamy construct.

So, monogamy or nonmonogamy?

Maybe the take-home lesson of the vast clinical and scientific literature tells us something we don't want to hear, especially from a self-help book: that there is no happy solution, no single sexual, social bonding, romantic love, and lust arrangement that quenches all our desires over the course of a lifetime. Perhaps conflict is imbedded into the human condition, resulting in our human struggles. Perhaps the only "solution" is to manage our struggles with dignity, good intentions, and healthy decisions, with compassion for ourselves, our partners, and our fellow humans.

Navigating Nonmonogamous Waters

If you are willing to try permitting or pursuing sex outside your primary relationship, the first thing to realize about nonmonogamy is that it generally means you can't lie or cheat. Maintaining honesty is likely to be extremely difficult, and in the end you may decide that the benefits are just not worth it. However, being upfront with your partner ensures that you will not destroy the love and trust you have.

Navigating the nonmonogamous waters can be a challenge for most of us. Theoretically, nonmonogamy means that both partners consent to allowing their partners to have sex with other people. If you and your mate originally came together as people seeking a nonmonogamous relationship, chances are good that you can collaborate as like-minded individuals seeking similar sexual encounters. However, if you and your mate had a traditional, monogamous relationship, and now one of you is aching to openly sleep with others, well . . . you are bound to have your hands full in making that transition.

One option is the "don't ask, don't tell" approach, in which one partner doesn't disclose while the other turns a blind eye. This is not an approach I'd recommend, however. In years past, many women, powerless to change their situation, had no choice but to look away while their husbands had affairs. I'm not remotely a proponent of this kind of arrangement, which has traditionally been rooted in patriarchy and the devaluation and economic and social oppression of women, leaving wives feeling that they had few options to object to their husbands' philandering because were unable to leave the marriage. Although some couples might find ways to make this kind of approach more fair and equitable, my concern is that hiding information puts couples on a slippery slope with "rules" that easily become an "excuse" for bad behavior—a license to cheat. Instead, today's nonmonogamous couples have come up with more open solutions.

There are umpteen versions of nonmonogamy, with the boundaries and framework varying in every conceivable way. In my experience nonmonogamous relationships are very difficult to make work but work best when they are *completely mutual*. The primary partner is not threatened and their primary position in the relationship is sacrosanct. For many couples, talking about adding a third lover can be a turn-on. But, as we've discussed earlier, everything changes when such a fantasy becomes reality.

Some nonmonogamous relationships limit the number of partners and restrict who those partners can be. There are often rules about "fluid bonding" that determine which partner(s) are allowed to engage in oral, anal, or vaginal sex without condoms. Some people agree to restrict the kinds of sexual acts you can have with others based on safe-sex precautions and boundaries about sexually intimacy. Some people have a rule that they will have no rules. Even if you agree to not have rules, consent, honesty, and expectations should be clear and not constantly shifting. Pick the arrangement that works best for you, and maintain the frame. As you contemplate which configuration is for you, make sure your motivations and actions have integrity. Now, more than ever, you'll need to keep your word and stay true to your intention.

Questions for you and your partner

As a therapist I would not advise nonmonogamy. Too complicated and too fraught. However, I do feel that it is my responsibility to offer some advice for how to approach this path if it's mutually agreed upon. As you explore creating your own nonmonogamous arrangements, consider the following questions based on my conversations with polyamory experts Drs. Geri Weitzman, Ken Haslam, and William Slaughter:

How would we like this nonmonogamous arrangement to go?

Based on who we are and where we are at today, how do we *expect* this will go?

What are our motivations?

What are our intentions?

How do we address emotional health and safety?

Which acts of sexuality and intimacy are permitted?

How do we schedule this?

Do we get involved with people we know and meet locally, or do we keep our actions with others all far away from our home?

Do we communicate with others via email or text, when we are home with each other, or do we constrict, restrict, and isolate our engagements with others?

What do we share with each other about our other partners, and what do we want and not want to know?

There is only one universal rule I would suggest regardless of your arrangement, and that is to respect your partners, both your primary partner and your new partners. Anticipate how they will all feel. Think about what you do and say because once it's said and the deed is done, it cannot be unsaid nor undone. Recognize that you and your partners are operating in

Are we interested in a fair and equitable sharing of each other
   with other lovers? Or are we deciding to be a mono-poly
   couple, in which only one of us is polyamorous and has sex
   with other people, while the other remains monogamous?
Are we committed to keeping our current relationship as our
   primary connection?
When we seek another lover, are we mainly interested in "new
   relationship energy," the sense of falling in love or lust?
Are we interested in building new lasting relationships? Do we
   want to cohabitate with our new partners?
Do we need to avoid the new partner(s) being primary or a
   constant lover?
How do we anticipate reckoning with our jealousies?
Can we feel happy for our long-term partner as they find lust and
   love from another (a feeling called *compersion*, which means
   feeling happy for your partner's sexual and romantic pleasures
   with another)?
What, if anything, do we tell each other about our experiences
   with others, and what do we tell relatives, friends, and
   children?
Are we willing to see an experienced therapist or mental health
   professional who can help us navigate these fraught waters?
   When do we need to seek such counsel?

relatively uncharted territory, fraught with fragile feelings and
easy resentments. Treat your partners with the utmost respect
and love, and keep your word and your promises.

RESPECT! That's the cardinal rule and the most likely predictor of any happy relationship.

chapter 13

Closing thoughts

The word *infidelity* comes from the word *infidel*, a heretic who turns his back on God. In certain periods in world history such a person received a death sentence. Our use of the same word for those who break the marital vow shows how judgmental we can be about marital infidelity. In this book I have taken what I hope is a more enlightened approach, one that combines understanding, forgiveness, change, atonement, and acceptance on all sides. As a psychiatrist I know that understanding, compassion, and love can help us with our conflicts and struggles. I also know that sometimes we need to hear the difficult answers and receive firm direction. As a therapist I can't simply hide behind the couch of compassion to avoid giving a direct answer. Certainly there are many unanswerable questions about infidelity, but here are a few questions that I wanted to address as honestly as I can before we close.

Can Long-Term Love Remain?

What a predicament we are in! We are filled with neurotransmitters and hormones honed through millions of years of evolution to seek out new partners, yet we yearn to be more than the sum of our biological directives. We all know that love is one of life's greatest gifts. At the same time, given our inherent conflicts, we wonder: Is lasting love possible?

Although there are many naysayers, psychoanalyst Steven A. Mitchell, PhD, author of *Can Love Last?* and psychologist Dorothy Tennov, PhD, author of *Love and Limerence: The Experience of Being in Love*, wrote scholarly books that offer hope for the romantic idealist, exploring the psychology of sustained, monogamous romance. Another optimist is Bianca Acevedo, PhD, a researcher at the University of California, Santa Barbara, in the Neuroscience Research Institute. With her colleagues, Dr. Acevedo has used brain scans to try to challenge the notion that infatuation and passion always devolves into a warm, fuzzy kind of love called *companion love*. She explored whether excitement and sexual desire can persist and, if so, whether there was evidence in the brain.

Dr. Acevedo concedes that the "uncertainty that ignites passion" does fade over time. The "emotional roller coasters and obsessive thinking that people often have in early stages of relationship, or even in later stages of relationships when things are uncertain" transforms once a couple is secure with each other, she explains. But what about that intense longing? Can that last? Now that we can look into the specific brain regions that get addicted to lust and love and now that we know from the animal models which brain chemicals and regions of the brain are involved in monogamous desire, can we find humans whose brains demonstrate the signs of such lasting, monogamous love, even after people have been married for over a decade?

Together with her colleagues Arthur Aron, Helen Fisher, and Lucy Brown, all noted experts in the field, Dr. Acevedo studied seventeen people who identified as still being in love after a minimum of ten years as a couple. Brain scans of these individuals showed neural activation patterns similar to those seen in individuals still in the heady romantic stage of new love *plus* more activation in areas rich in opioid receptors, serotonin receptors, and the classical oxytocin/vasopressin receptors. So, according to this small brain study, monogamy and romantic love can last. According to Dr. Acevedo, the top predictor of keeping long-term love is "holding your partner in high regard and thinking positive thoughts about them." I couldn't agree more.

Is It Ever Okay to Cheat?

This is a tricky question. Nothing is simple in matters of love and family. If you feel compelled to lie about your behaviors, as much as I'd caution against it, I recognize that you must have your reasons. If you really can't reconcile your differences with your spouse, consider divorce, or at least a trial separation. Hopefully you'll find a way to avoid that.

Staying married takes hard work. If you're reading this book, then you're probably the kind of person who is willing to do the kind of work that sustaining a relationship requires. But not all people are willing. Some couples are content with a "don't ask, don't tell" policy, and some spouses say, "I'd rather not know."

I started this book talking about my father seeking refuge with other women, and I'll end with him as well. After my wonderful sister became severely mentally ill, there was always fighting in my home. Many times my father threatened to leave. Once, when I was about ten, my dad did leave the house for a few days after threatening divorce. I recall those terrible days when I cried and couldn't concentrate at school. Partly out of compassion for me, my dad returned home. Had my father permanently left the marriage and moved out—as most divorced fathers did in the 1960s—my life would have been very different, and not for the better. My poor sister was schizophrenic. My devoted mother was beside herself with emotional pain that left her helpless at times. My father grieved. I was the youngest of the family, but my parents relied on me even as a youngster. Because of all that was expected of me, I couldn't leave home even after I began college. God knows what would have happened to me—and them—if my father had left our home.

My parents were loving people with the best of intentions who did everything possible for me, but they were at war with reality. My sister's mental illness was not something they could accept, nor could they reconcile their marital differences openly and honestly. Like many families, my family lived with painfully evident secrets.

Now, many years later, I find myself in the position of offering information and advice about infidelity as well as the need to be honest and to address life on life's terms. Yet I realize there are no simple, one-size-fits-all answers. Although it is easy to tell other people what they should do, it's hard to walk in their shoes. I know that every person, every couple, every family needs to find their own way. I know that every life is uniquely complicated, our actions are inevitably contradictory, and our lives can be painful and cut painfully short.

But if it seems even remotely possible, please take away from this book the idea that acceptance, honesty, and avoiding infidelity can be the keys to a fulfilling relationship. Only in an honest relationship can we find what we seem to want the most: to be truly known by another and loved for who we really are.

Recommitting to Emotional Fidelity

Not too long ago churches and synagogues used to require that engaged couples attend classes before marriage. Some still do. There, in the context of the spiritual teaching, religious leaders talk about family, love, lust, sex, and even monogamy. Nowadays more and more people fall in love, live together, and then tie the knot later, with little counsel or forethought to the significance of the marriage commitment. They recite vows at their wedding that they often soon forget. Perhaps now more than ever, given all the increased opportunities for infidelity, how you plan your life together and work to maintain your vows are critically important.

Keeping your word and holding up your end of the bargain is important to any relationship. If you are a soldier in the army and secretly work for a hostile, foreign power, you may face a firing squad. If you lie to your boss and disregard your employment contract, you will most likely ultimately get caught, get fired, and destroy everything you've worked for. My point is this: you can't expect to act in such a treasonous way toward your spouse without serious fallout.

Even beyond being true to your word about sex, devotion to your partner is among the most important ingredients of a committed relationship—in other words, *emotional fidelity*. No business can function, no partnership can endure, no friendship can last if the partners can't trust each other. Emotional fidelity is at the core of every good relationship, particularly your marriage.

Here are some vows of emotional fidelity. They are vows for making a long-term commitment like marriage. They are the promise of putting the relationship first and safeguarding that connection as your most precious asset.

Vows of emotional fidelity

I promise that . . .

   . . . you can trust that I will be there for you.

   . . . I will put you first above others. Just after the needs of the children, your welfare will be my priority.

   . . . I will have your back.

   . . . I will create opportunities for you to feel great pleasure and love.

   . . . you can trust me to know you, that my word and intentions are good.

   . . . I will endeavor, within reason, to mitigate your hardships.

   . . . I dedicate myself to the intention, however imperfectly executed, that nothing will tear us apart, and everything will bring us closer.

Notice that nowhere in these Vows of Emotional Fidelity are you *asking* for anything. Everywhere you are *giving*. After years of *too much water under the bridge,* couples often focus on what they are not *getting* instead of focusing on what they should be *giving*. This is a vow of giving, not getting. The irony of love is that you ensure your happiness not by taking, demanding, or even asking—you ensure your happiness by giving.

Because of the contradictory desires embedded in our human nature, infidelity is a common vexing aspect of being human. In the preceding pages I have tried to use knowledge, honesty, and decency to help you prevail over our human failings, knowing all the time that this is an overwhelming task and that we all fall short sometimes. When it comes to love and lust, what feels right is often so terribly wrong, and what feels urgent and liberating is programmed by our DNA and can't easily be overcome with rational thought. At the very least I hope this book has helped you to better understand the complexities of this struggle and to recognize that your personal troubles with infidelity are neither original nor easily solved. I urge you, dear reader, to be compassionate toward yourself and others and to remember that sustained romantic love is worth the struggle. It is as close as we get to the divine.

appendix:
for more help

Sometimes infidelity is the tip of the iceberg. If you are a cheating partner, your infidelity is occasionally the consequence of depression, anxiety, narcissism, attention deficit disorder, a mood disorder, or even a love and sex addiction. If you are a betrayed partner, the discovery that your partner has been unfaithful may lead you to develop a posttraumatic stress disorder, adjustment disorder, anxiety disorder, or depression. These are situations that call for professional guidance. If you ask me, even if you suffer no psychological ailments, a good licensed therapist or trained clergy may be an invaluable guide during the discovery of and recovery from infidelity.

For assistance, the best place to start is with your trusted sources of guidance. For those who belong to a spiritual group, religious leaders may have excellent local resources. If you feel too embarrassed to reach out to them directly—although they have heard it all before and you are not the first!—you could try an anonymous call to the national headquarters of your religious denomination. If professional psychological help is what you are looking for, ask for a referral from your family physician or from the psychology or psychiatry department at your nearby medical center. Nonprofit, university-based medical centers are particularly reliable. For more extensive listings of licensed professionals and general information about mental health problems, here are just a few of the many national organizations, with information taken from their websites, that may offer information about psychological ailments and may provide guidance when seeking a licensed therapist.

American Association of Marriage and Family Therapists
www.aamft.org/iMIS15/AAMFT/Content/directories/locator_terms_of_use.aspx
Marriage and family therapists are highly qualified professionals trained to diagnose and treat a wide range of serious clinical problems, including depression, marital problems, anxiety, individual psychological problems, and child-parent problems.

American Psychiatric Association
www.psychiatry.org
The American Psychiatric Association is an organization of psychiatrists working together to ensure humane care and effective treatment for all persons with mental illness, including substance use disorders. It is the voice and conscience of modern psychiatry. Its vision is a society that has available, accessible, quality psychiatric diagnosis and treatment.

American Psychological Association
www.apa.org
APA is the leading scientific and professional organization representing psychology in the United States, with more than 115,700 researchers, educators, clinicians, consultants, and students as its members. Its mission is to advance the creation, communication, and application of psychological knowledge to benefit society and improve people's lives.

IITAP
www.iitap.com
Patrick J. Carnes, PhD, is the founder of the International Institute for Trauma and Addiction Professionals (IITAP). Since its inception IITAP's vision has been to be a premier training resource for therapists specializing in the areas of addiction recovery and trauma.

ASECT
www.asect.net
The Association of Sexuality Educators, Counselors and Therapists (ASECT) is a nonprofit national organization aimed at associating the

medical practitioners interested and involved in the field of sexual medicine. It mainly aims to disseminate scientific knowledge to practitioners to enhance their basic understanding in human sexuality and help improve their clinical acumen, providing a platform for the exchange of knowledge, information, and technology in the vast and relatively unexplored field of sexual medicine.

This is far from an exhaustive list, but with the help of the internet, you can find the support you need rather quickly. Professional help could save your marriage, if that's what you want. More importantly, it can save your life, enabling you to survive and thrive.

acknowledgments

First and foremost, thanks are due to my patients, who consistently inspire me with their bravery to face their truth in order to become better people.

When I first decided to put some of my ideas down on paper, Alexander Morgan provided invaluable editorial assistance. Bruce Roseman, Kristina Bicher, Ellen Roseman, Bette Clark, Martin Sherry, Michele Galen, and my toughest critics, my children Alexander and Claire Rosenberg, provided vital early feedback. Although I've cited on the preceding pages many colleagues who have influenced my work, I've not directly mentioned many of my unsung heroes. That list is long and includes Drs. David Preven, Eslee Samberg, Philip Wilner, Laura Feder, Harris (and Ilka) Peck, Richard Francis, Robert Millman, Anne Beeder, Robert Michels, Hazel Weinberg, Charles Silberstein, Richard Kogan, Carol Weiss, Michael Pearlman, Ken Adams, Robert Weiss, the faculties of the psychiatry department of the Cornell Weill Medical Center and Payne Whitney Clinic, and my colleagues at the American Psychiatric Association, the International Institute for Trauma and Addiction Professionals, the Society for Sex Therapy and Research, and the Association for Addiction Psychiatry.

In addition, I want to thank Suzanne O'Connor, Tami Ver-Helst, Jeff Berzon, Sam Decker, Celia Marie Freitas, and Tom W. Smith, PhD, senior fellow at the National Opinion Research Center at the University of Chicago. I am indebted to the diversity of mental health experts who spoke to me, from my colleagues in the sex addiction community, to those who work in the clergy, to those who write about and counsel people in the polyamory community.

I cannot possibly and sufficiently thank my "book doctor," editor, and coach—a brilliant writer in her own right—Jessica DuLong. This book would not have been possible without the tireless conceptual inspiration, guidance, and support from my agent, Joy Tutela at the David Black Agency, and the catalytic and enthusiastic dedication from my editor, Dan Ambrosio at Da-Capo Press and Hachette Publishing. Impeccable fact checking and the preparation of the references was done by the esteemed neuropsychologist and researcher Bianca Acevedo, PhD. A review of the manuscript was performed by my close friend and an eminent neuroscientist Todd Sacktor, MD.

I am very grateful to Lynn Novick, who supported me and graciously acted as a sounding board throughout the writing of this book. Thanks are always due to my inspirational siblings, Gail Zitin, Robert Zitin, and Merle Rosenberg, and to my mom and dad, who gave me life and taught me how to live it. Last but not least, in this book I discuss how to survive and thrive against adversity, and adversity touches us all. No one has personally taught me more about what it means to survive, thrive, and love than my children, Claire and Alexander.

notes

introduction

xi   **nothing can be changed until it is faced:** James Baldwin, *The Cross of Redemption: Uncollected Writings* (New York: Vintage, 2011).

xi   ***The Archaeology of Medical Perception:*** Michel Foucault, *The Birth of the Clinic* (New York: Routledge, 2012).

xi   **much more like us than different:** Robert J. Ursano, "'More Simply Human Than Otherwise': Harry S. Sullivan's 'Conceptions of Modern Psychiatry': The First William Alanson White Memorial Lectures (Published 1940)," *Psychiatry* 75, no. 1 (2012): 1–2.

xvii **save people from *normal* unhappiness:** Sigmund Freud and Josef Breuer, *Studies in Hysteria*, trans. Nicola Luckhurst (London: Penguin Books, 2004).

Part One—Biology and the Basics

chapter 1. The basics of a cheating heart

4   **trust of a committed relationship:** Olivia Ann Leeker and Al Carlozzi, "Effects of Sex, Sexual Orientation, Infidelity Expectations, and Love on Distress Related to Emotional and Sexual Infidelity," *Journal of Marital and Family Therapy* 40, no. 1 (2014): 68–91; Pieternel Dijkstra, Dick P. H. Barelds, and Hinke A. K. Groothof, "Jealousy in Response to Online and Offline Infidelity: The Role of Sex and Sexual Orientation," *Scandinavian Journal of Psychology* 54, no. 4 (August 2013): 328–336.

4   **the greatest threats to their union:** W.-Y. Shieh, "Why Same-Sex Couples Break Up: A Follow-Up Study in Taiwan," *Journal of GLBT Family Studies* 12, no. 3 (May 2016): 257–276.

7   **be the root of much unhappiness:** A. J. Kposowa, "Divorce and Suicide Risk," *Journal of Epidemiology and Community Health* 57, no. 12 (2003): 993; Ingeborg Rossow, "Suicide, Alcohol, and Divorce: Aspects of Gender and Family Integration," *Addiction* 88, no. 12 (December 1993): 1659–1665; D. Olbrich and J. Bojanovsky, "Psychiatric Hospitalization of Divorced Persons," *Psychiatria Clinica* 14, no. 1 (1981): 56–65; S. B. Scott, G. K. Rhoades, S. M. Stanley, E. S. Allen,

and H. J. Markman, "Reasons for Divorce and Recollections of Pre-marital Intervention: Implications for Improving Relationship Education," *Couple and Family Psychology* 2, no. 2 (June 2013): 131–145; Justin T. Denney, Richard G. Rogers, Patrick M. Krueger, and Tim Wadsworth, "Adult Suicide Mortality in the United States: Marital Status, Family Size, Socioeconomic Status, and Differences by Sex," *Social Science Quarterly* 90, no. 5 (December 2009): 1167.

7   **first step toward resolving them:** A. J. Hawkins, B. J. Willoughby, and W. J. Doherty, "Reasons for Divorce and Openness to Marital Reconciliation," *Journal of Divorce & Remarriage* 53, no. 6 (2012): 453–463.

7   **admitted to cheating on their partner:** Survey on Cheating, YouGov, May 27–29, 2015, https://d25d2506sfb94s.cloudfront.net/cumulus_uploads/document/9uudxvfiae/tabs_OPI_infidelity_20150529.pdf.

7   **a partner after discovering infidelity:** Ibid.

8   **upset by infidelity (32 vs. 34 percent):** D. A. Frederick and M. R. Fales, "Upset Over Sexual versus Emotional Infidelity Among Gay, Lesbian, Bisexual, and Heterosexual Adults," *Archives of Sexual Behavior* 45, no. 1 (January 2016): 175–191.

8   **more likely to cheat than Americans:** Richard Wike, "French More Accepting of Infidelity Than People in Other Countries," Pew Research Center, January 14, 2014, www.pewresearch.org/fact-tank/2014/01/14/french-more-accepting-of-infidelity-than-people-in-other-countries.

8   **being the peak periods for cheating:** Effrosyni Adamopoulou, "New Facts on Infidelity," *Economics Letters* 121, no. 3 (December 2013): 458–462.

8   **65 percent view it as unforgivable:** Sesen Negash, Ming Cui, Frank D. Fincham, and Kay Pasley, "Extradyadic Involvement and Relationship Dissolution in Heterosexual Women University Students," *Archives of Sexual Behavior* 43, no. 3 (April 2014): 531–539.

8   **spoke freely about their transgressions:** Rebecca J. Brand, Charlotte M. Markey, Ana Mills, and Sara D. Hodges, "Sex Differences in Self-Reported Infidelity and Its Correlates," *Sex Roles* 57, no. 1–2 (July 2007): 101–109.

8   **over the past twenty-four years:** "The General Social Survey," GSS, http://gss.norc.org.

9   **estimated 90 percent of divorces:** Michael J Rosenfeld, "Who Wants the Breakup? Gender and Breakup in Heterosexual Couples," in *Social Networks and the Life Course*, ed. Duane Alwin, Diane Felmlee, and Derek Kreager (New York: Springer Press, forthcoming).

9   **infidelity today than in the 1970s:** Smith, "General Social Survey."

9   **rising to the level of young adult men:** Monica T. Whitty and Laura-Lee Quigley, "Emotional and Sexual Infidelity Offline and in Cyberspace," *Journal of Marital and Family Therapy* 34, no. 4 (October 2008): 461–468; Al Cooper, "Sexuality and the Internet: Surfing into the New Millennium," *Cyber Psychology and Behavior* 1, no. 2 (January 1998): 187–193; Kimberly S. Young, "Internet Sex Addiction: Risk Factors, Stages of Development, and Treatment," *American Behavioral Scientist* 52, no. 1 (September 2008): 21–37.

9   **young, the middle aged, and seniors:** M. Mullinax, K. J. Barnhart, K. Mark, D. Herbenick, "Women's Experiences with Feelings and Attractions for Someone Outside Their Primary Relationship," *Journal of Sex and Marital Therapy* 42, no. 5 (July 2016): 431–447.

10   **educated and less well-off women:** David C. Atkins, Donald H. Baucom, and Neil S. Jacobson, "Understanding Infidelity: Correlates in a National Random Sample," *Journal of Family Psychology* 15, no. 4 (2001): 735–749.

10   **church or religious institutions cheat more:** Kelly Campbell and David W. Wright, "Marriage Today: Exploring the Incongruence Between Americans' Beliefs and Practices," *Journal of Comparative Family Studies* (2010): 329–345.

10   **men and women are most likely to cheat:** Bruce Elmslie and Edinaldo Tebaldi, "So, What Did You Do Last Night? The Economics of Infidelity," *Kyklos* 61, no. 3 (August 2008): 391–410.

13   **excited by visual cues, including porn:** Gert Martin Hald, "Gender Differences in Pornography Consumption Among Young Heterosexual Danish Adults," *Archives of Sexual Behavior* 35, no. 5 (October 2006): 577–585.

13   **ever before, to remedy sexual boredom:** Kristen P. Mark, E. Janssen, and Robin R. Milhausen, "Infidelity in Heterosexual Couples: Demographic, Interpersonal, and Personality-Related Predictors of Extradyadic Sex," *Archives of Sexual Behavior* 40, no. 5 (2011): 971–982.

16   **favored patterns for our actions:** Martin Bellander, Rasmus Berggren, Johan Mårtensson et al., "Behavioral Correlates of Changes in Hippocampal Gray Matter Structure During Acquisition of Foreign Vocabulary," *Neuroimage* 131 (May 2016): 205–213.

17   **New York City's sex trafficking business:** NYC Mayor's Office to Combat Domestic Violence, "New York City Domestic Violence Fatality Review Committee: 2016 Annual Report," 2016, www1.nyc.gov/assets/ocdv/downloads/pdf/2016-frc-report.pdf.

18   **part of the brain called the *amygdala*:** Larry Cahill, Melina Uncapher, Lisa Kilpatrick, Mike T. Alkire, and Jessica Turner, "Sex-Related Hemispheric Lateralization of Amygdala Function in Emotionally

Influenced Memory: An FMRI Investigation," *Learning and Memory* 11, no. 3 (May 2004): 261–266.

chapter 2. Desire: The engine of the affair

19   **free of needless drama and conflict:** L. Bloch, C. M. Haase, and R. W. Levenson, "Emotion Regulation Predicts Marital Satisfaction: More Than a Wives' Tale," *Emotion* 14, no. 1 (February 2014): 130–144.

20   **sex for under six minutes:** M. D. Waldinger, P. Quinn, M. Dilleen, R. Mundayat, D. H. Schweitzer, and M. Boolell, "A Multinational Population Survey of Intravaginal Ejaculation Latency Time," *Journal of Sexual Medicine* 2, no. 4 (July 2005): 492–497.

20   **from roughly ten to twenty seconds:** S. Kratochvíl, "The Duration of Female Orgasm," *Ceskoslovenska Psychiatrie* 89, no. 5 (October 1993): 296–299.

21   **the 1979 book *Disorders of Desire*:** Helen Singer Kaplan, *The Sexual Desire Disorders: Dysfunctional Regulation of Sexual Motivation* (New York: Psychology Press, 1995).

23   **making us taller, healthier, and smarter:** P. K. Joshi, T. Esko, H. Mattsson et al., "Directional Dominance on Stature and Cognition in Diverse Human Populations," *Nature* 523, no. 7561 (July 23, 2015): 459–462.

24   **complications in fertility and pregnancy:** Christing E. Garver-Apgar, Steven W. Gangestad, Randy Thornhill, Robert D. Miller, and Jon J. Olp, "Major Histocompatibility Complex Alleles, Sexual Responsivity, and Unfaithfulness in Romantic Couples," *Psychological Science* 17, no. 10 (May 2006): 830–835.

24   **genes in the MHC had more affairs:** Jan Havlicek and S. Craig Roberts, "MHC-Correlated Mate Choice in Humans: A Review," *Psychoneuroendocrinology* 34, no. 4 (May 2009): 497–512; C. Wedekind and S. Füri, "Body Odour Preferences in Men and Women: Do They Aim for Specific MHC Combinations or Simply Heterozygosity?" *Proceedings of the Royal Society B: Biological Sciences* 264, no. 1387 (1997): 1471–1479.

25   **copulate repeatedly until sexual exhaustion:** Frank A. Beach and Lisbeth Jordan, "Sexual Exhaustion and Recovery in the Male Rat," *Quarterly Journal of Experimental Psychology* 8, no. 3 (July 1956): 121–133.

25   **President Calvin Coolidge and his wife:** The Coolidge joke goes like this: While touring a farm, First Lady Grace Coolidge noticed a rooster mating frequently. When she asked how often that happened, the attendant answered, "Dozens of times each day." Mrs. Coolidge said, "Tell that to the president when he comes by." The

president then took the same tour, and was informed of the rooster's frequent mating habits. Upon hearing that, the president asked, "Same hen every time?" The reply was, "Oh, no, Mr. President, a different hen every time." President: "Tell that to Mrs. Coolidge."

25   **phylogenetic spectrum, from beetles to primates:** Donald A. Dewsbury, "Effects of Novelty of Copulatory Behavior: The Coolidge Effect and Related Phenomena," *Psychological Bulletin* 89, no. 3 (1981): 464; Sandra Steiger, Ragna Franz, Anne-Katrin Eggert, and Josef K. Müller, "The Coolidge Effect, Individual Recognition and Selection for Distinctive Cuticular Signatures in a Burying Beetle," *Proceedings of the Royal Society B: Biological Sciences* 275, no. 1645 (2008): 1831–1838.

25   *nucleus accumbens* **and** *ventral tegmental area:* Tiffany M. Love, "Oxytocin, Motivation and the Role of Dopamine," *Pharmacology Biochemistry and Behavior* 119 (April 2014): 49–60.

25   **as its reward/reinforcement center:** D. F. Fiorino, A. Coury, and A. G. Phillips, "Dynamic Changes in Nucleus Accumbens Dopamine Efflux During the Coolidge Effect in Male Rats," *Journal of Neuroscience.* 17, no. 12 (June 1997): 4849–4855.

26   **think about sex ten times a day:** Terri D. Fisher, Zachary T. Moore, and Mary-Jo Pittenger, "Sex on the Brain?: An Examination of Frequency of Sexual Cognitions as a Function of Gender, Erotophilia, and Social Desirability," *Journal of Sex Research* 49, no. 1 (January 2012): 69–77.

27   **offering her name and phone number:** D. G. Dutton and A. P. Aron, "Some Evidence for Heightened Sexual Attraction Under Conditions of High Anxiety," *Journal of Personality and Social Psychology* 30, no. 4 (October 1974): 510–517.

32   **while having sex with their partners:** Janniko R. Georgiadis, A. A. T. Simone Reinders, Anne M. J. Paans, Remco Renken, and Rudie Kortekaas, "Men versus Women on Sexual Brain Function: Prominent Differences During Tactile Genital Stimulation, but Not During Orgasm," *Human Brain Mapping* 30, no. 10 (October 2009): 3089–3101.

33   **ensure the survival of the species:** Stuart J. Ritchie, Simon R. Cox, Xueyi Shen et al., "Sex Differences in the Adult Human Brain: Evidence from 5,216 UK Biobank Participants," *bioRxiv* 123729 (April 2017): https://doi.org/10.1101/123729.

34   **new gene products in the brain:** Debbie Hampton, "How Your Thoughts Change Your Brain, Cells and Genes," *Huffington Post,* March 23, 2016, www.huffingtonpost.com/debbie-hampton/how-your-thoughts-change-your-brain-cells-and-genes_b_9516176.html.

chapter 3. Sex and love: The primordial addictions

38   **enables us to know right from wrong:** Andrew B. Barron, Elrik Sø-
      vik, and Jennifer L. Cornish, "The Roles of Dopamine and Related
      Compounds in Reward-Seeking Behavior Across Animal Phyla,"
      Frontiers in Behavioral Neuroscience 4 (October 2010): 163.

39   **first mammals appeared on earth:** T. B. Rowe, T. E. Macrini, and
      Z. X. Luo, "Fossil Evidence on Origin of the Mammalian Brain,"
      Science 332, no. 6032 (May 2011): 955–957; John Hawks, "How Has
      the Human Brain Evolved?," *Scientific American*, 2013, www.scientific
      american.com/article/how-has-human-brain-evolved.

40   **people experience romantic yearning:** Helen E. Fisher, Xiaoment
      Xu, Arthur Aron, and Lucy L. Brown, "Intense, Passionate, Roman-
      tic Love: A Natural Addiction? How the Fields That Investigate Ro-
      mance and Substance Abuse Can Inform Each Other," *Frontiers in
      Psychology* 7 (May 2016): 687.

44   **which he called the *death instinct*:** Arnold M. Cooper, "The
      Narcissistic-Masochistic Character," in *Contemporary Psychoanaly-
      sis in America: Leading Analysts Present Their Works*, ed. Arnold M.
      Cooper, 111–132 (Washington, DC: American Psychiatric Publishing,
      2006).

46   **naturally produce more sex hormones:** Katherine L. Goldey and
      Sari M. van Anders, "Sexual Thoughts: Links to Testosterone and
      Cortisol in Men," *Archives of Sexual Behavior* 41, no. 6 (December
      2012): 1461–1470.

46   **roughly 1 to 3 percent each year:** S. M. Harman, E. J. Metter, J. D.
      Tobin, J. Pearson, M. R. Blackman, and Baltimore Longitudinal
      Study of Aging, "Longitudinal Effects of Aging on Serum Total and
      Free Testosterone Levels in Healthy Men: Baltimore Longitudinal
      Study of Aging," *Journal of Clinical Endocrinology and Metabolism* 86,
      no. 2 (February 2001): 724–731; Henry A. Feldman, Christopher
      Longcope, Carol A. Derby et al., "Age Trends in the Level of Serum
      Testosterone and Other Hormones in Middle-Aged Men: Longi-
      tudinal Results from the Massachusetts Male Aging Study," *Journal
      of Clinical Endocrinology and Metabolism* 87, no. 2 (February 2002):
      589–598; Roger D. Stanworth and T. Hugh Jones, "Testosterone for
      the Aging Male: Current Evidence and Recommended Practice,"
      Clinical Interventions in Aging 3, no. 1 (March 2008): 25–44.

46   **levels drop precipitously after menopause:** Dana R. Ambler, Eric
      J. Bieber, and Michael P. Diamond, "Sexual Function in Elderly
      Women: A Review of Current Literature," *Reviews in Obstetrics and
      Gynecology* 5, no. 1 (2012): 16–27.

46   **increase testosterone in some people:** Katherine L. Goldey, Lanice
      R. Avery, and Sari M. van Anders, "Sexual Fantasies and Gender/
      Sex: A Multimethod Approach with Quantitative Content Analysis

and Hormonal Responses," *Journal of Sex Research* 51, no. 8 (November–December 2014): 917–931.

46 **during high-energy or stressful events:** Goldey and van Anders, "Sexual Thoughts."

46 **fuels the brain's reward system:** Susan K. Putnam, Jianfang Du, Saturo Sato, and Elaine M. Hull, "Testosterone Restoration of Copulatory Behavior Correlates with Medial Preoptic Dopamine Release in Castrated Male Rats," *Hormones and Behavior* 39, no. 3 (May 2001): 216–224.

46 **club members participated in group sex:** Michelle J. Escasa, Jacqueline F. Casey, and Peter B. Gray, "Salivary Testosterone Levels in Men at a U.S. Sex Club," *Archives of Sexual Behavior* 40, no. 5 (October 2001): 921–926.

47 **very deep and physiological level:** Ibid.

49 **simultaneously decreasing our sexual arousal:** C. M. Meston and P. F. Frohlich, "The Neurobiology of Sexual Function," *Archives of General Psychiatry* 57, no. 11 (November 2000): 1012–1030; T. H. Krüger, P. Haake, U. Hartmann, M. Schedlowski, and M. S. Exton, "Orgasm-Induced Prolactin Secretion: Feedback Control of Sexual Drive?" *Neuroscience and Biobehavioral Reviews* 26, no. 1 (January 2002): 31–44.

50 **called the *dorsal ventral pallidum*:** M. M. Lim and L. J. Young, "Vasopressin-Dependent Neural Circuits Underlying Pair Bond Formation in the Monogamous Prairie Vole," *Neuroscience* 125, no. 1 (January 2004): 35–45; L. A. O'Connell and H. A. Hofmann, "Evolution of a Vertebrate Social Decision-Making Network," *Science* 336, no. 6085 (May 2012): 1154–1157.

51 **monogamy and infidelity in animals:** K. C. Berridge and M. L. Kringelbach, "Pleasure Systems in the Brain," *Neuron* 86, no. 3 (2015): 646–664.

51 **other animals throughout their lives:** Larry J. Young, "The Neural Basis of Pair Bonding in a Monogamous Species: A Model for Understanding the Biological Basis of Human Behavior," in *Offspring: Human Fertility Behavior in Biodemographic Perspective*, ed. Kenneth W. Wachter and Rodolfo A. Bulatao, 91–103 (Washington, DC: National Academies Press, 2003).

51 **and the associated nucleus accumbens:** Miranda M. Lim, Zuoxin Wang, Daniel E. Olazábal et al., "Enhanced Partner Preference in a Promiscuous Species by Manipulating the Expression of a Single Gene," *Nature* 429, no. 6993 (June 2004): 754.

52 **enough to bond these voles for life:** Hui Wang, Florian Duclot, Yan Liu, Zuoxin Wang, and Mohammed Kabbaj, "Histone Deacetylase Inhibitors Facilitate Partner Preference Formation in Female Prairie Voles," *Nature Neuroscience* 16, no. 7 (July 2013): 919–924.

54   **the brain containing vasopressin receptors:** O'Connell and Hofmann, "Evolution of a Vertebrate Social Decision-Making Network."

54   **poor social bonding in childhood:** Hasse Walum, Lars Westberg, Susanne Henningsson et al., "Genetic Variation in the Vasopressin Receptor 1a Gene (AVPR1A) Associates with Pair-Bonding Behavior in Humans," *Proceedings of the National Academy of Sciences* 105, no. 37 (September 2008): 14153–14156; Hasse Walum, Paul Lichtenstein, Jenae M. Neiderhiser et al., "Variation in the Oxytocin Receptor Gene Is Associated with Pair-Bonding and Social Behavior," *Biological Psychiatry* 71, no. 5 (March 2012): 419–426.

56   **predict whether a relationship will last:** Inna Schneiderman, Orna Zagoory-Sharon, James F. Leckman, and Ruth Feldman, "Oxytocin During the Initial Stages of Romantic Attachment: Relations to Couples' Interactive Reciprocity," *Psychoneuroendocrinology* 37, no. 8 (August 2012): 1277–1285.

56   **vole research, was the area that "lit up.":** D. Scheele, A. Wille, K. M. Kendrick et al., "Oxytocin Enhances Brain Reward System Responses in Men Viewing the Face of Their Female Partner," *Proceedings of the National Academy of Sciences* 110, no. 50 (December 2013): 20308–20313.

56   **where romantic thoughts seem to reside:** Bianca P. Acevedo, Arthur Aron, Helen E. Fisher, and Lucy L. Brown, "Neural Correlates of Long-Term Intense Romantic Love," *Social Cognitive and Affective Neuroscience* 7, no. 2 (February 2012): 145–159.

57   **of drug addicts suffering withdrawal:** Fisher et al., "Intense, Passionate, Romantic Love."

Part II—The Taste for New Sex

chapter 4. Cyber relationships and America's obsession with porn

64   **internet's inherent compulsion loop:** Vance Packard, *The Hidden Persuaders* (New York: Penguin, 1982).

64   **so potent—a dopamine multiplier:** Jonathan Williams and Eric Taylor, "Dopamine Appetite and Cognitive Impairment in Attention Deficit/Hyperactivity Disorder," *Neural Plasticity* 11, no. 1–2 (January 2004): 115–132.

64   **upon which academics tend to agree:** Ogi Ogas and Sai Gaddam, *A Billion Wicked Thoughts: What the Internet Tells Us About Sexual Relationships* (London: Penguin, 2011).

65   **internet instead of the street corner:** E. Argento, M. Taylor, J. Jollimore et al., "The Loss of Boystown and Transition to Online Sex

Work: Strategies and Barriers to Increase Safety Among Men Sex Workers and Clients of Men," *American Journal of Men's Health* (June 2016).

66   **intentionally viewed or downloaded porn:** Julie M. Albright, "Sex in America Online: An Exploration of Sex, Marital Status, and Sexual Identity in Internet Sex Seeking and Its Impacts," *Journal of Sex Research* 45, no. 2 (April–June 2008): 175–186.

66   **most spouses to be an act of infidelity:** Ana J. Bridges, Raymond M. Bergner, and Matthew Hesson-McInnis, "Romantic Partners' Use of Pornography: Its Significance for Women," *Journal of Sex and Marital Therapy* 29, no. 1 (January 2003): 1–14.

66   **that lead to impairment or distress.":** Aviv Weinstein, Laura Curtiss Feder, Kenneth Paul Rosenberg, and Pinhas Dannon, "Internet Addiction Disorder: Overview and Controversies," in *Behavioral Addictions: Criteria, Evidence, and Treatment,* ed. Kenneth Paul Rosenberg and Laura Curtiss Feder, 99–117 (New York: Academic Press, 2014).

66   **arousal, attraction, and sexual performance:** Brian Y. Park, Gary Wilson, Jonathan Berger et al., "Is Internet Pornography Causing Sexual Dysfunctions? A Review with Clinical Reports," *Behavioral Sciences* 6, no. 3 (September 2016): 17.

67   **sexual satisfaction and sexual intimacy.":** A. M. Weinstein, R. Zolek, A. Babkin, K. Cohen, and M. Lejoyeux, "Factors Predicting Cybersex Use and Difficulties in Forming Intimate Relationships Among Male and Female Users of Cybersex," *Frontiers in Psychiatry* 6 (January 2015): 54.

67   **about their partner's use of such material.":** Bridges, Bergner, and Hesson-McInnis, "Romantic Partners' Use of Pornography."

68   **billion video views on their site that year:** "Pornhub's 2016 Year in Review," Pornhub Insights, January 4, 2017. www.pornhub.com/insights/2016-year-in-review.

68   **the site's most popular search term overall:** Kurt Schlosser, "Pornhub Reveals, State by State, Its Most Popular Search Terms Among U.S. Users," GeekWire, March 2, 2016, www.geekwire.com/2016/pornhub-most-searched-terms.

68   **orgasm and male sexual performance.":** Léa J. Séguin, Carl Rodrigue, and Julie Lavigne, "Consuming Ecstasy: Representations of Male and Female Orgasm in Mainstream Pornography," *Journal of Sex Research* (July 2017): 1–9.

69   **little else seems to matter to the brain:** Mihaly Csikszentmihalyi and Isabella Selega Csikszentmihalyi, Optimal Experience: Psychological Studies of Flow and Consciousness (Cambridge: Cambridge University Press, 2000).

72 **They will never win.":** Kristian Daneback, Al Cooper, and Sven-Axel Månsson, "An Internet Study of Cybersex Participants," *Archives of Sexual Behavior* 34, no. 3 (June 2005): 321–328.

73 **accessible way to meet potential new partners.":** Mark D. Griffiths, "Cyber Affairs—A New Area for Psychological Research," *Psychology Review* 7, no. 1 (September 2000): 28–31.

83 **stopped publishing pictures of nude women:** Amy O'Leary, "So How Do We Talk About This?" *New York Times*, May 9, 2012, www .nytimes.com/2012/05/10/garden/when-children-see-internet -pornography.html.

chapter 5. The emotional affair

86 **associated with love, desire, and validation:** Acevedo et al., "Neural Correlates of Long-Term Intense Romantic Love."

87 **of people as all good or all bad:** M. C. Zanarini, J. L. Weingeroff, and F. R. Frankenburg, "Defense Mechanisms Associated with Borderline Personality Disorder," *Journal of Personality Disorders* 23, no. 2 (2009): 113–121.

88 **in greater flux than ever before:** Richard Bulcroft, Kris Bulcroft, Karen Bradley, and Carl Simpson, "The Management and Production of Risk in Romantic Relationships: A Postmodern Paradox," *Journal of Family History* 25, no. 1 (July 2016): 63–92.

89 **more upset by a physical one:** Whitty and Quigley, "Emotional and Sexual Infidelity Offline and in Cyberspace."

89 **resource reallocation among women:** Victoria Thornton and Alexander Nagurney, "What Is Infidelity? Perceptions Based on Biological Sex and Personality," *Psychology Research and Behavior Management* 4 (May 2011): 51–58.

89 **men focused on extramarital sex:** Joh Sabini and Melanie C. Green, "Emotional Responses to Sexual and Emotional Infidelity: Constants and Differences Across Genders, Samples, and Methods," *Personality and Social Psychology Bulletin* 30, no. 11 (July 2004): 1375–1388.

90 **more contingent on romantic commitment.":** Jamie L. Goldenberg, Mark J. Landau, Tom Pyszczynski et al., "Gender-Typical Responses to Sexual and Emotional Infidelity as a Function of Mortality Salience Induced Self-Esteem Striving," *Personality and Social Psychology Bulletin* 29, no. 12 (July 2003): 1585–1595.

90 **about what each individual values:** Thornton and Nagurney, "What Is infidelity?"

90 **value on sex overall felt less distress:** Goldenberg et al., "Gender-Typical Responses to Sexual and Emotional Infidelity as a Function of Mortality Salience Induced Self-Esteem Striving."

90 **women progress into physical ones:** Shirley Glass, *Not "Just Friends": Rebuilding Trust and Recovering Your Sanity After Infidelity* (New York: Free Press, 2007).

91 **are discontented with their partners:** Elizabeth S. Allen and Galena K. Rhoades, "Not All Affairs Are Created Equal: Emotional Involvement with an Extradyadic Partner," *Journal of Sex and Marital Therapy* 34, no. 1 (2008): 51–65.

chapter 6. The sex quest for threesomes and orgies

93 **fantasies may or may not reassure you:** Ashley E. Thompson and E. Sandra Byers, "Heterosexual Young Adults' Interest, Attitudes, and Experiences Related to Mixed-Gender, Multi-Person Sex," *Archives of Sexual Behavior* 46, no. 3 (April 2017): 813–822.

94 **but also dangerous and destructive:** E. R. Pinta, "Pathological Tolerance," *American Journal of Psychiatry* 135, no. 6 (June 1978): 698–701.

95 **cheating behind their partners' backs:** Mark Oppenheimer, "Married, with Infidelities," *New York Times*, June 30, 2011, www.nytimes.com/2011/07/03/magazine/infidelity-will-keep-us-together.html.

95 **had participated in a threesome:** Thompson and Byers, "Heterosexual Young Adults' Interest, Attitudes, and Experiences Related to Mixed-Gender, Multi-Person Sex."

96 **at a large southeastern university:** H. Morris, I. J. Chang, and D. Knox, "Three's a Crowd or Bonus?: College Students' Threesome Experiences," *Journal of Positive Sexuality* 2 (November 2016).

96 **threesome than reported by women.":** Ibid.

96 **percentage of women say the same:** Christian C. Joyal, Amélie Cossette, and Vanessa Lapierre, "What Exactly Is an Unusual Sexual Fantasy?" *Journal of Sexual Medicine* 12, no. 2 (February 2015): 328–340; "The Truth About Threesomes," *Cosmopolitan*, July 19, 2010, www.cosmopolitan.com/sex-love/advice/a3271/threesome-statistic.

97 **same-sexed and mixed-sex configurations:** Morris, Chang, and Knox, "Three's a Crowd or Bonus?"

97 **drug abuse as well as risky investments:** Camelia M. Kuhnen and Joan Y. Chiao, "Genetic Determinants of Financial Risk Taking," *PLoS One* 4, no. 2 (2009): e4362.

98 **of vulnerability to addictive diseases.":** Mary Jeanne Kreek, David A. Nielsen, Eduardo R. Butelman, and K. Steven LaForge, "Genetic Influences on Impulsivity, Risk Taking, Stress Responsivity and Vulnerability to Drug Abuse and Addiction," *Nature Neuroscience* 8, no. 11 (November 2005): 1450–1457.

98 **dopamine genes tend to seek unusual sex:** Jonathan Benjamin, Lin Li, C. Patterson, Benjamin D. Greenberg, Dennis L. Murphy,

and Dean H. Hamer, "Population and Familial Association Between the D4 Dopamine Receptor Gene and Measures of Novelty Seeking," *Nature Genetics* 12, no. 1 (January 1996): 81–84.

99 **dopamine genes had more one-night stands:** Justin R. Garcia, James MacKillop, Edward L. Aller, Ann M. Merriwether, David Sloan Wilson, and J. Koji Lum, "Associations Between Dopamine D4 Receptor Gene Variation with Both Infidelity and Sexual Promiscuity," *PLoS One* 5, no. 11 (November 2010): e14162.

100 **people often have ADD problems:** Martin P. Kafka and R. A. Prentky, "Attention-Deficit/Hyperactivity Disorder in Males with Paraphilias and Paraphilia-Related Disorders: A Comorbidity Study," *Journal of Clinical Psychiatry* 59, no. 7 (1998): 388–396.

chapter 7. When pain is pleasure, and other kink

106 **hints of domination or submission:** Christian C. Joyal, "Defining 'Normophilic' and 'Paraphilic' Sexual Fantasies in a Population-Based Sample: On the Importance of Considering Subgroups," *Journal of Sexual Medicine* 3, no. 4 (December 2015): 321–330.

106 **US women report having used a vibrator:** Debra Herbenick, Michael Reece, Stephanie Sanders, Brian Dodge, Annahita Ghassemi, and J. Dennis Fortenberry, "Prevalence and Characteristics of Vibrator Use by Women in the United States: Results from a Nationally Representative Study," *Journal of Sexual Medicine* 6, no. 7 (2009): 1857–1866.

107 **"hysteria" (now known as anxiety):** Katherine Angel, "The History of 'Female Sexual Dysfunction' as a Mental Disorder in the 20th Century," *Current Opinion in Psychiatry* 23, no. 6 (November 2010): 536–541; Rachel P. Maines, *The Technology of Orgasm: "Hysteria," the Vibrator, and Women's Sexual Satisfaction* (Baltimore, MD: Johns Hopkins University Press, 2001).

109 **experience and can stop it at any time:** Elena Faccio, Claudia Casini, and Sabrina Cipolletta, "Forbidden Games: The Construction of Sexuality and Sexual Pleasure by BDSM 'Players'," *Culture, Health, and Sexuality* 16, no. 7 (2014): 752–764.

109 **partner after the BDSM experience:** Dana R. Ambler, Eric J. Bieber, and Michael P. Diamond, "Sexual Function in Elderly Women: A Review of Current Literature," *Reviews in Obstetrics and Gynecology* 5, no. 1 (2012): 16–27; Brad J. Sagarin, Ellen M. Lee, and Kathryn Rebecca Klement, "Sadomasochism Without Sex? Exploring the Parallels Between BDSM and Extreme Rituals," *Journal of Positive Sexuality* 1 (November 2015): 32–36; Kathryn Rebecca Klement, Ellen M. Lee, James K. Ambler et al., "Extreme Rituals in a BDSM

Context: The Physiological and Psychological Effects of the 'Dance of Souls'," *Culture Health and Sexuality* 19, no. 4 (2017): 453–469.

110 **they're often with us for a lifetime:** Maines, *The Technology of Orgasm.*

112 **experiences contribute to our sexuality:** J. D. Fortenberry, "Puberty and Adolescent Sexuality," *Hormones and Behavior* 64, no. 2 (July 2013): 280–287.

114 **the nineteenth and twentieth century:** Richard von Krafft-Ebing, *Psychopathia Sexualis: With Especial Reference to Antipathic Sexual Instinct: A Medico-Forensic Study* (New York: Rebman, 1904).

115 **roles between tops and bottoms:** J. E. Rehor, "Sensual, Erotic, and Sexual Behaviors of Women from the 'Kink' Community," *Archives of Sexual Behavior* 44, no. 4 (2015): 825–836.

115 **being watched naked or having sex:** Ibid.

Part III—Discovery, Disclosure, and Moving Forward Toward Healing

chapter 8. Discovery: The truth comes out—what now?

125 **first step of your hero's journey:** Patrick Carnes, *A Gentle Path Through the Twelve Steps: The Classic Guide for All People in the Process of Recovery* (Center City, MN: Hazelden Publishing, 2012).

130 **system prepares us for action:** Sandra L. Bloom and Brian J. Farragher, *Destroying Sanctuary: The Crisis in Human Service Delivery Systems* (Oxford: Oxford University Press, 2010).

131 **hormones norepinephrine and cortisol:** J. D. Bremner, "Traumatic Stress: Effects on the Brain," *Dialogues in Clinical Neuroscience* 8, no. 4 (2006): 445–461.

131 **survive and have a chance for growth:** J. C. Markowitz, J. Lipsitz, and B. L. Milrod, "Critical Review of Outcome Research on Interpersonal Psychotherapy for Anxiety Disorders," *Depression and Anxiety* 31, no. 4 (April 2014): 316–325.

134 **acting out, it is called *pain shopping*:** Stephanie Carnes, *Mending a Shattered Heart: A Guide for Partners of Sex Addicts* (Carefree, AZ: Gentle Path Press, 2011).

chapter 9. Disclosure: Prepare yourself for the messiness

147 **likely to end nonmarital relationships:** M. J. Rosenfeld, R. J. Thomas, and M. Falcon, "How Couples Meet and Stay Together," Stanford University, September 22, 2009, https://data.stanford .edu/hcmst; M. F. Brinig, D. W. Allen, "'These Boots Are Made for

Walking': Why Most Divorce Filers Are Women," *American Law and Economics Review* 2, no. 1 (2000): 126–169.

chapter 10. Emotional healing

170 **report being happy with their spouses:** Atkins, Baucom, and Jacobson, "Understanding Infidelity"; Glass, *Not "Just Friends"*; Hara Estroff Marano, "From Promise to Promiscuity," *Psychology Today*, July 3, 2012, www.psychologytoday.com/articles/201207/promise -promiscuity.

171 **bad decisions in their own lives:** Eric Berne, *Games People Play: The Psychology of Human Relationships* (San Francisco: Grove Press, 1964).

172 **lonelier and worry that they matter less:** Brian Beach and Sally-Marie Bamford, "Isolation: The Emerging Crisis for Older Men. A Report Exploring Experiences of Social Isolation and Loneliness Among Older Men in England" (Independent Age and the International Longevity Center, United Kingdom, 2014), www.independent age.org/sites/default/files/2016-05/isolation-the-emerging-crisis -for-older-men-report.pdf.

172 **bad advice was the norm:** Roy Spalding, Toni Schindler Zimmerman, Christine A. Fruhauf, James H. Banning, and Joanna Pepin, "Relationship Advice in Top-Selling Men's Magazines: A Qualitative Document Analysis," *Journal of Feminist Family Therapy* 22, no. 3 (2010): 203–224.

173 **fulfillment than the search for El Dorado.":** Peter D. Kramer, *Should You Leave?: A Psychiatrist Explores Intimacy and Autonomy—and the Nature of Advice* (New York: Scribner, 1997).

173 ***Emotionally Focused Therapy for Couples:*** Leslie S. Greenberg and Susan M. Johnson, *Emotionally Focused Therapy for Couples* (New York: Guilford Press, 2010).

chapter 11. Sexual healing and fidelity

179 **meaning their sexual self turns off:** Patrick J. Carnes, *Sexual Anorexia: Overcoming Sexual Self-Hatred* (New York: Simon and Schuster, 2009).

184 **weeks to three months, and that's all:** Kenneth Paul Rosenberg, Patrick Carnes, and Suzanne O'Connor, "Evaluation and Treatment of Sex Addiction," *Journal of Sex & Marital Therapy* 40, no. 2 (2014): 77–91.

189 **having them stare into each other's eyes:** Arthur Aron, Edward Melinat, Elaine N. Aron, Robert Darrin Vallone, and Renee J. Bator, "The Experimental Generation of Interpersonal Closeness: A Procedure and Some Preliminary Findings," *Personality and Social Psychology Bulletin* 23, no. 4 (July 1997): 363–377.

190   **wound up marrying six months later!:** Ibid.

chapter 12. Sex and love with more than one:
Do open relationships work?

210   **she saw as a trend away from monogamy:** Lauren Peterson, "Wanting Monogamy as 1,946 Men Await My Swipe," *New York Times*, May 26, 2017, www.nytimes.com/2017/05/26/style/modern-love-wanting-monogamy-as-1946-men-await-your-swipe.html?mcubz=1.

218   **tests, however, the storyline fell apart:** Alexander G. Ophir, Steven M. Phelps, Anna Bess Sorin, and Jerry O. Wolff, "Social but Not Genetic Monogamy Is Associated with Greater Breeding Success in Prairie Voles," *Animal Behaviour* 75, no. 3 (2008): 1143–1154.

218   **went back to her established partner.":** Walum et al., "Variation in the Oxytocin Receptor Gene Is Associated with Pair-Bonding and Social Behavior"; Ophir et al., "Social but Not Genetic Monogamy Is Associated with Greater Breeding Success in Prairie Voles"; H. Ledford, "'Monogamous' Vole in Love-Rat Shock," *Nature* 451, no. 7179 (2008): 617.

219   **have higher levels of testosterone:** Sari M. van Anders, Lisa Dawn Hamilton, and Neil V. Watson, "Multiple Partners Are Associated with Higher Testosterone in North American Men and Women," *Hormones and Behavior* 51, no. 3 (March 2007): 454–459.

220   **the world's male population today:** Tatiana Zerjal, Yali Xue, Giorgio Bertorelle et al., "The Genetic Legacy of the Mongols," *American Journal of Human Genetics* 72, no. 3 (2003): 717–721.

chapter 13. Closing thoughts

228   **classical oxytocin/vasopressin receptors:** Acevedo et al., "Neural Correlates of Long-Term Intense Romantic Love."